ZICKZACK
neu

1

Paul Rogers, Lawrence Briggs, Bryan Goodman-Stephens

Nelson

Thomas Nelson and Sons Ltd
Nelson House   Mayfield Road
Walton-on-Thames   Surrey
KT12 5PL   UK

51 York Place
Edinburgh
EH1 3JD   UK

Thomas Nelson (Hong Kong) Ltd
Toppan Building 10/F
22A Westlands Road
Quarry Bay   Hong Kong

Thomas Nelson Australia
102 Dodds Street
South Melbourne   Victoria 3205
Australia

Nelson Canada
1120 Birchmount Road
Scarborough   Ontario
M1K 5G4   Canada

First published by Thomas Nelson & Sons Ltd 1993

ISBN 0-17-439785-2
NPN 9 8 7 6 5 4 3 2 1

Printed in Great Britain

Acknowledgements

Deutsche Bundesbank
Österreichische Nationalbank
Schweizerische Nationalbank
Oxford University Press
Rodillian High School, Wakefield
Städtisches Gymnasium, Eschweiler
Städtisches Gymnasium, Gütersloh
Familie Ostkamp
Werner Franken
Klaus May
Josef Pogadl
Benjamin Spencer

Photography

David Simson
David and Diane Collett

Illustration

Judy Byford
Sean Crawford
Karen Donnelly
Matthew Doyle
Diane Fisher
Helen Holroyd
Louise Jackson
Julia King
Lotty
Julian Mosedale
Mal Peet
Jude Wisdom
Jackie Rough
Nick Sharatt
Peter Smith
Kate Taylor
Dennis Tinkler
Jo Wright

Every effort has been made to trace the copyright holders of extracts reprinted in this book. We apologis for any inadvertent omission, which can be rectified i subsequent reprint.

Welcome to ZickZack neu!

You are about to set off on a course that will take you through German-speaking countries throughout the world and will help you to understand and enjoy using German yourself. ● ● ● For much of the time you will be working on activities with guidance from your teacher, but at the end of each chapter there is a section called **sb** *Selbstbedienung*, where you'll be able to choose for yourself activities at different levels. ● ● ● If you want to take your time and check that you've understood, choose GOLD activities. If you're ready to try out what you've already learned, choose ROT activities. If you want to stretch yourself still further, then the SCHWARZ activities are for you. For all three types of activity, you can ask your teacher for answer sheets so that you can check how you're getting on. ● ● ● At the back of the book you can look up words or phrases that you've forgotten or don't understand and find extra help with grammar. You'll find English translations of the **sb** *Selbstbedienung* instructions, too.

Viel Spaß und mach's gut!

	Seite

Kapitel 1 Hallo! Wie heißt du? — **6**

Lernziel 1 – Hallo! Ich heiße … (Greetings and giving your name)

Lernziel 2 – Wieviel? Eins bis zwanzig (Counting to 20)

Lernziel 3 – Wie alt bist du? (Saying your age and using the German alphabet)

Kapitel 2 Wo wohnst du? — **16**

Lernziel 1 – Länder in Europa (Some countries in Europe)

Lernziel 2 – Wo ich wohne (Saying where you live)

Lernziel 3 – Wo liegt das? (Saying where places are)

Kapitel 3 Meine Familie — **26**

Lernziel 1 – Hast du Geschwister? (Talking about brothers and sisters)

Lernziel 2 – Das ist meine Familie (Introducing your family)

Lernziel 3 – Hast du ein Haustier? (Talking about pets)

Kapitel 4 Bei mir zu Hause — **36**

Lernziel 1 – Ich wohne in … (Saying where your house or flat is)

Lernziel 2 – Die Zimmer (Rooms in the house)

Lernziel 3 – Telefonnummern und Adressen (Telephone numbers, addresses, numbers 21-100)

Kapitel 5 Mein Alltag — **46**

Lernziel 1 – Wie spät ist es? (Telling the time)

Lernziel 2 – Tagesroutine (Daily routine)

Lernziel 3 – Daten und Feiertage (Dates and special celebrations)

Kapitel 6 Wie schmeckt's? — **56**

Lernziel 1 – Was ißt du zum Frühstück? (Breakfast)

Lernziel 2 – Mittagessen und Abendessen (Midday and evening meals)

Lernziel 3 – Gesundes Essen (Healthy eating)

Kapitel 7 Schule — **66**

Lernziel 1 – Schulfächer und Schulaufgaben (School subjects)

Lernziel 2 – Lieblingsfächer (Likes and dislikes of subjects; opinions)

Lernziel 3 – Der Schultag (School day and routine)

Seite

Kapitel 8 Meine Freizeit　　**76**

Lernziel 1 – Sport und Hobbys (Sports and hobbies)

Lernziel 2 – Fernsehen (Expressing opinions about television programmes)

Lernziel 3 – Was machst du am liebsten? (Favourites)

Kapitel 9 Was kostet das?　　**86**

Lernziel 1 – Geld und Preise ((Money and prices; changing money)

Lernziel 2 – Ich habe Hunger! (Snacks, drinks and ice creams)

Lernziel 3 – Was machst du mit deinem Geld? (What you spend your money on or are saving up for)

Kapitel 10 Wie schön!　　**96**

Lernziel 1 – Wie ist das Wetter? (The weather and the seasons)

Lernziel 2 – Was machst du in den Ferien? (Holidays)

Lernziel 3 – Meint ihr uns? (Agreeing/disagreeing with German young people's impressions of Britain)

Wo spricht man Deutsch?　　**108**

Maps to show in which parts of the world people speak German

Grammatik: Überblick　　**110**

A summary of the grammar in Stage 1

Was ist im Wörterbuch?　　**126**

Help with using a dictionary

Wörterliste: Deutsch – Englisch　　**128**

A German – English vocabulary

Wörterliste: Englisch – Deutsch　　**136**

An English – German vocabulary

Glossar　　**144**

English translations of instructions in this book

Lernziel 1

Hallo! Ich heiße ...

 **Hallo!**

Hör gut zu. Was sagen sie?

1 Hallo! Ich bin Anne.

2 Hallo! Ich bin Renate.

3 Grüß dich! Ich bin Paul.

4 Hallo! Ich heiße Uschi.

5 Grüß Gott! Ich bin Martin.

6 Grüß dich! Ich bin Oliver.

7 Guten Tag! Ich bin Frau Meyer.

8 Guten Morgen! Ich heiße Stefan.

Im Sportklub

Hör gut zu.
Schreib die Namen in der richtigen Reihenfolge auf.
Beispiel
1 *Boris*

Partnerarbeit

A – Was sagt Anne?
B – Hallo! Ich bin Anne.
A – Gut.
B – Was sagt Renate?
A – ...

Elke

Gabi

Sven

Barbara

Martin

Boris

Fotoquiz

Hier sind sechs Teenager.
Hör gut zu. Was sagen sie?

Hier sind die Babyfotos von den Teenagern.

Ich heiße Susi.

Ich bin Sven.

Ich bin Brigitte.

Ich bin Lutz

Ich bin Bernd.

Ich heiße Christa.

 Partnerarbeit. Wer ist das?

A – Nummer eins, ist das Lutz?
B – Nein, das ist Susi.
A – Nummer zwei, ist das ...?
B – Ja, das ist ...

 Namenlied

Hör zu und sing mit.

Tip des Tages

Hallo!
Grüß dich!
Grüß Gott!

Guten Tag!
Guten Morgen!

Wie heißt du?
Ich bin ...
Ich heiße ...

Wer ist das?
Das ist Lutz.

Hallo Mutter, hallo Vater!
Tag Andreas, Tag Renate!
Hallo Thomas, hallo Tina!
Grüß dich Georg, grüß dich Grete,
grüß dich Gabi!

Lernziel 2
Wieviel?
Eins bis zwanzig

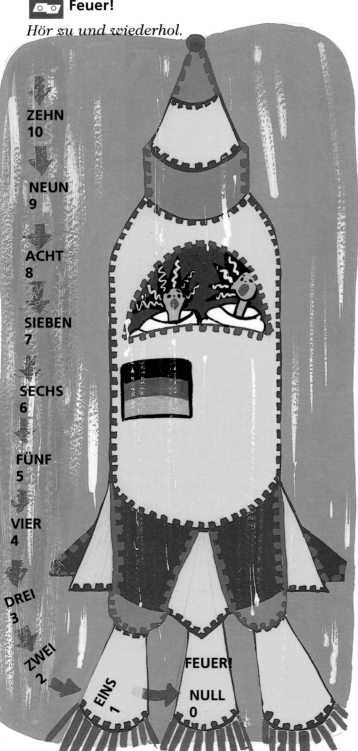

Feuer!

Hör zu und wiederhol.

ZEHN
10

NEUN
9

ACHT
8

SIEBEN
7

SECHS
6

FÜNF
5

VIER
4

DREI
3

ZWEI
2

EINS
1

FEUER!

NULL
0

Partnerarbeit. Was ist das?

A – Was ist das?
B – Neun.

1 7 19 12 3 16 11 14 2 20 9 4 18 10 8 17 5 15 13 6

Was läuft?

Hör gut zu.
Schreib die Saalnummern
in der richtigen Reihenfolge auf.
Beispiel
Saal 7
Saal …

KINO · CENTER LICHTBURG
Kaiserstraße 74 ⚡ 233070
Saal:

1 BAMBI
2 Der Tunnel
3 TOM und JERRY
4 Tarzan
5 Simon SEZ in N.Y.
6 Fantasia
7 FEUER

▱ Die Hitparade

Hör zu.

1	Wie heißt du?	Polizei
2	Gute Nacht	Elegy
3	Wie geht's?	Simon Sez
4	He, du da	Ede Funk
5	Telefonliebe	Britta Tell
6	Ich geh ins Bett	Serpentine
7	Mann oh Mann	Ozean
8	Anne	Hallo
9	Teenage Rock	Head Bangers Inc.
10	Komm mit!	Prima

11	Grüß dich!	Hanno H.
12	Toll Toll Toll	O Weh
13	Queen of Hearts	The Gamblers
14	Die Sonne scheint	Karussell
15	Blitz	Evi Bamm
16	Susi ist erst siebzehn	Hbf.
17	Broken Dreams	Insomniacs
18	Einmal ist keinmal	Frei
19	Schwarz Rot Gold	Lola Lace
20	Sieben Tage	Feuerwerk

◖◗ Partnerarbeit

A – Was ist auf Platz drei?
B – ‚He, du da' von Ede Funk.
A – Nein, das ist auf Platz vier.

Zahlreich

Schreib die richtigen Zahlen auf.

Beispiel
A *acht*

Tip des Tages

Die Zahlen von 0 bis 20:

0	null		
1	eins	11	elf
2	zwei	12	zwölf
3	drei	13	dreizehn
4	vier	14	vierzehn
5	fünf	15	fünfzehn
6	sechs	16	sechzehn
7	sieben	17	siebzehn
8	acht	18	achtzehn
9	neun	19	neunzehn
10	zehn	20	zwanzig

Lernziel 3

Wie alt bist du?

🔲⊙⊙ **Wie heißt du? Wie alt bist du?**

Hör zu.
Schreib die Namen in der richtigen Reihenfolge auf. Wie alt sind sie?

Anne   Anja   Asaf   Sven

Paul   Fatima   Thomas   Karin

Was sagen Asaf und Anne?

Wähl einen Namen. Wie heißt du? Wie alt bist du? Frag einen Partner/eine Partnerin.

Wie heißt du?

Asaf. Und du?

Anne. Wie alt bist du?

Ich bin vierzehn. Und du?

Ich bin siebzehn Jahre alt.

Oh, ...

◖◗ Partnerarbeit. Was sagen sie?

Frag einen Partner/eine Partnerin.

1   2   12   15   3   14   4   20

Frank   Britta   Elke   Dani

Beispiel

A – Was sagt Nummer eins?
B – Ich heiße Frank. Ich bin zwölf Jahre alt.

Tip des Tages

Wie alt bist du?
Ich bin ... (Jahre alt).

Partnerarbeit. Wie alt sind sie?

*Was meinst du? Frag deinen Partner/
deine Partnerin.*

A – Detlev?
B – 14 Jahre alt, oder?
A – Nein, 16 Jahre alt.

Florian

Heike

Detlev

Lisa

Markus

 *Hör jetzt zu. Die richtigen Antworten
sind auf Kassette.*

Wie schreibt man das?

Wie heißt du?	
Wapnewski	
Wap-? Was? Wie schreibt man das?	
W-A-P-N-E-W-S-K-I	

Tip des Tages

– Wie heißt du?
– Trudeau.
– Wie schreibt man das?
– T-R-U-D-E-A-U.

Internationales Leichtathletikfest

Hör gut zu. Schreib die Namen fertig.

Beispiel
1 *S. Mayer*

100-Meter-Lauf Frauen

1 S. Maye __   D
2 D. Smit __   GB
3 C. Jacquema __ __   F
4 R. Ni __ __ __   USA
5 T. Lundq __ __ __ __   S
6 B. Piag __ __   CH
7 H.-J. Be __ __ __ __ __ LIE
8 M. Wald __ __ __ __   A

sb ▸ *Selbstbedienung*

Lernziel 1

Buchstabensalat

Was ist das?

Beispiel
1 *hallo*

Lernziel 1

Spiegelbild

Wer ist das? Schreib den Namen.

Beispiel
1 *Susi*

Lernziel 2

Wieviel ist das?

Beispiel
a *Sechs und eins – das ist sieben.*

Lernziel 2

 Welche Zahl ist das?

Welcher Buchstabe ist …

… in 1 aber nicht in 13 ☐

… in 2 und 4 aber nicht in 6 ☐

… in 2 und 9 ☐

… in 7 aber nicht in 1 ☐

… in 2, 10 und 12 ☐

… in 11 aber nicht in 12 ☐

… in 8 und in 10 ☐

… in 1 aber nicht in 2? ☐

Welche Zahl ist das?

Lernziel 3

 Zahlenrätsel

Welches Wort ist das?
Beispiel
1 *hallo*

1 zwei   sechs   fünf   fünf   neun .

2 vierzehn   zwölf   acht / zwei
acht   zwölf   siebzehn   elf /
fünfzehn   sieben ?

3 vierzehn   zwölf   acht /sechs
fünf   elf / sechzehn   zwölf
dreizehn   elf / fünfzehn   sieben ?

Schlüssel	9	=	o
1 = r	10	=	n
2 = h	11	=	t
3 = m	12	=	i
4 = g	13		s
5 = l	14		w
6 = a	15		d
7 = u	16		b
8 = e	17		ß

Jetzt bist du dran!
Schreib ein Zahlenrätsel.

Lernziel 3

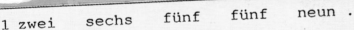 **Frage und Antwort**

Finde die richtigen Antworten.

Was ist auf Platz sieben in der Hitparade**?**

Wieviel ist das**?**

Was läuft im Saal zwei**?**

Was sagt Paul**?**

Ich bin zwölf.

Neun.

Wie alt bist du**?**

Grüß dich!

Der Tunnel.

Mann oh Mann.

Bildvokabeln

Im Klassenraum

- die Tafel
- das Fenster
- die Landkarte
- die Tür
- die Leinwand
- die Lehrerin
- der Tageslichtprojektor
- das Bücherregal
- der Kassettenrecorder
- der Stuhl
- der Schüler
- der Tisch
- der Kuli
- das Lineal
- das Buch
- der Schulranzen
- der Bleistift
- das Heft

 **Alphabetlied**

Hör zu und sing mit.

A B C D, so fängt's an.
E F G H geht es dann.
I J K
L und M!
So geht das Alphabet.
So geht …
das Alphabet.

N O P Q, hör gut zu.
R S T U, ich und du.
V W X
Y Z!
So geht das Alphabet.
So geht …
das Alphabet.

1 Greetings

Hallo!	*Hello*
Grüß dich!	*Hi (there)*
Grüß Gott!	*Hello (in Southern Germany, Austria and Switzerland)*
Guten Tag!	*Hello*
Guten Morgen!	*Good morning*

2 Asking questions

Wie heißt du?	*What's your name?*
Wie alt bist du?	*How old are you?*
Wie schreibt man das?	*How do you spell that?*

3 Talking about yourself

Ich bin …	*I am …*
Ich heiße …	*My name is …*
Ich bin dreizehn (Jahre alt).	*I am thirteen (years old).*

4 Numbers from 0 to 20

Die Zahlen von 0 bis 20

0	null		
1	eins	11	elf
2	zwei	12	zwölf
3	drei	13	dreizehn
4	vier	14	vierzehn
5	fünf	15	fünfzehn
6	sechs	16	sechzehn
7	sieben	17	siebzehn
8	acht	18	achtzehn
9	neun	19	neunzehn
10	zehn	20	zwanzig

Lernziel 1

Länder in Europa

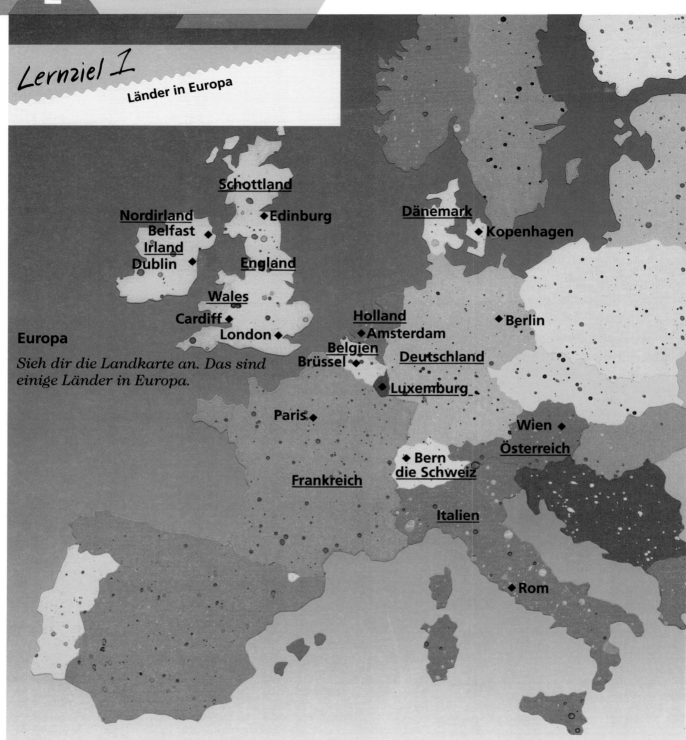

Europa

*Sieh dir die Landkarte an. Das sind
einige Länder in Europa.*

Schottland
◆ Edinburg
Nordirland
Belfast ◆
Irland
Dublin ◆
England
Wales
Cardiff ◆
London ◆
Dänemark
◆ **Kopenhagen**
Holland
◆ **Amsterdam**
◆ **Berlin**
Belgien
Brüssel ◆
Deutschland
◆ **Luxemburg**
Paris ◆
Wien ◆
Österreich
◆ **Bern**
die Schweiz
Frankreich
Italien
◆ **Rom**

Partnerarbeit. Welches Land ist das?

A – Welches Land ist das? F–R–A–...
B – Frankreich?
A – Richtig! Jetzt bist du dran.
B – Welches Land ist das? D–E–...?

**Partnerarbeit.
Was ist die Hauptstadt?**

A – Was ist die Hauptstadt von Belgien?
B – Brüssel.
A – Richtig.

🎞 Auf dem Campingplatz

Diese Teenager sind im Urlaub in Deutschland.
Hör zu. Wer spricht? Schreib die Namen in der richtigen
Reihenfolge auf. Woher kommen sie?

Beispiel
1 *Nicole. Aus der Schweiz.*

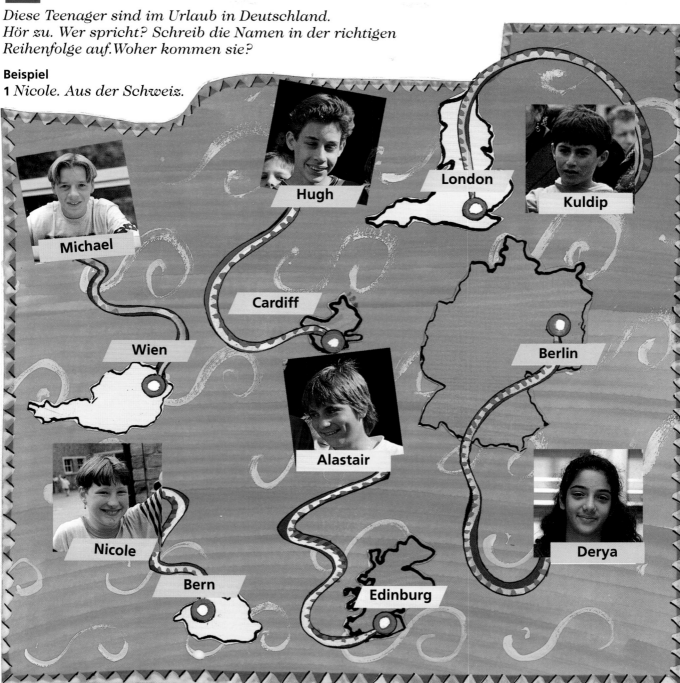

Hugh

London

Kuldip

Michael

Cardiff

Wien

Berlin

Alastair

Nicole

Derya

Bern

Edinburg

◖◗ Partnerarbeit. Wer bin ich?

Sieh dir die Personen und die Landkarten an.
Wähl eine Person. Wer bist du? Dein(e) Partner(in) muß raten.

Beispiel
A – Ich komme aus Deutschland. Wer bin ich?
B – (Du bist) Derya.
A – Richtig.

Tip des Tages

Woher kommst du?	
Ich komme aus	Deutschland. Wales. Irland. der Schweiz.

Lernziel 2
Wo ich wohne

Ich heiße Michael.
Ich komme aus
Deutschland.
Ich wohne in …

Ich heiße Andy.
Ich komme aus Schottland.
Ich wohne in …

Ich heiße David.
Ich komme aus Wales.
Ich wohne in …

Ich heiße Helga.
Ich komme aus der Schweiz.
Ich wohne in …

Ich heiße Kim.
Ich komme aus England.
Ich wohne in …

Ich heiße Ingrid.
Ich komme aus Deutschland.
Ich wohne in …

Partnerarbeit. Ich wohne in Köln

Sieh dir die Fotos und Bilder an.
Was sagen die Jungen und Mädchen?

Beispiel
A – Was sagt Michael?
B – Ich heiße Michael. Ich komme aus Deutschland. Ich wohne in Köln.

Steffi

Wo ich wohne

Hör zu und sing mit.

1.
Ich wohne hier,
Du wohnst da.
Ich sage ‚Nein',
Und du, du sagst ‚Ja'.

Doch ich wohne
Im selben Ort, wo du wohnst,
Und er heißt die Welt,
Er heißt die Welt.

2.
Ich sage ‚Komm!'
Du sagst ‚Geh!'
Ich schreibe A,
Und du, du schreibst B.

Doch ich wohne
Im selben Ort, wo du wohnst,
Und er heißt die Welt,
Er heißt die Welt.

3.
Ich bin jung,
Du bist alt.
Ich sage ‚Los!'
Und du, du sagst ‚Halt!'

Doch ich wohne
Im selben Ort, wo du wohnst,
Und er heißt die Welt,
Er heißt die Welt.

Wer ist das?

Sieh dir das Bild und die Fragen und Antworten an. Wer ist das?

Woher kommst du? — Aus Salzburg in Österreich

Wie alt bist du? — Sieben

Was machst du? — Ich schreibe meine Symphonie Nummer 1

Zungenbrecher

Kannst du das sagen? Hör zu und wiederhol.

Doris ist Deutsche und kommt aus Dortmund.
Erich und Friedrich kommen aus Zürich.
Konrad, Karin, Kirsten und Kurt kommen aus Köln.
Gerold und Berthold kommen aus Detmold.

Kannst du andere Zungenbrecher schreiben?

Tip des Tages

Wo wohnst du?	
Ich wohne in	Neukirchen.
	Salzburg.
	Bern
	Belfast.
	Dublin.
	Newcastle.

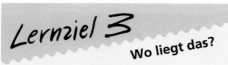

Lernziel 3

Wo liegt das?

 Wo wohne ich?

Sieh dir die Landkarte an und hör gut zu.
Wo wohnen die acht Jungen und Mädchen?

Beispiel
1 *München*

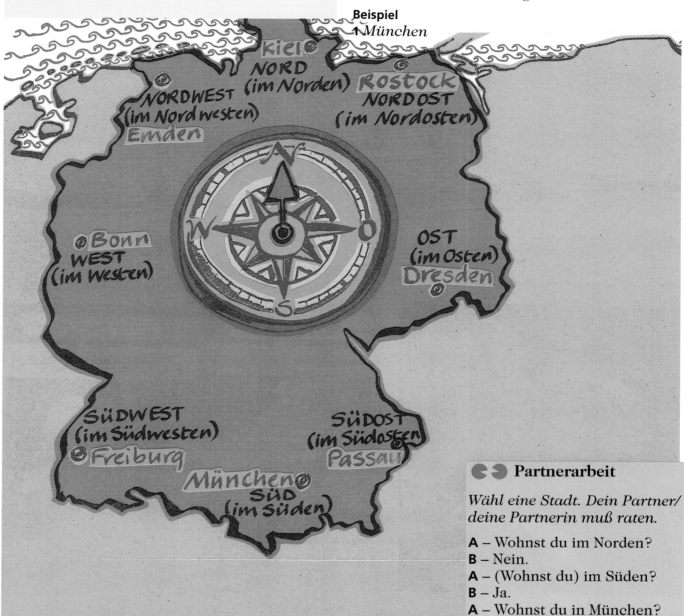

Partnerarbeit

Wähl eine Stadt. Dein Partner/
deine Partnerin muß raten.

A – Wohnst du im Norden?
B – Nein.
A – (Wohnst du) im Süden?
B – Ja.
A – Wohnst du in München?
B – Ja. Jetzt bist du dran.

Das liegt im Osten

Hör gut zu, und sieh dir die Tabellen an.
Wo wohnen die sechs Teenager?

Beispiel
1 *Alima – Hamburg – im Norden.*

A		
Alima	Peter	Jutta
Martin	Heidi	Kasimir

B		
Köln	Saarbrücken	Hamburg
Chemnitz	München	Berlin

C		
im Süden	im Westen	im Nordosten
im Norden	im Osten	im Südwesten

Richtig oder falsch?

*Sieh dir die Landkarte an, und hör gut zu.
Ist das richtig oder falsch?*

Beispiel
1 *Richtig*

HAMBURG

Petra

Rellingen

Gommern

Rudi

MAGDEBURG

Dirk

Stefan   Siegburg

Deutschland

DRESDEN

BONN

Ulli

Monika

Österreich

Peggau

Baden   ZÜRICH   Zirl

Ingrid

die Schweiz   INNSBRUCK   GRAZ

Partnerarbeit. Wo liegt Zirl?

*Sieh dir die Landkarte nochmal an, und stell
deinem Partner/deiner Partnerin Fragen.*

Beispiel

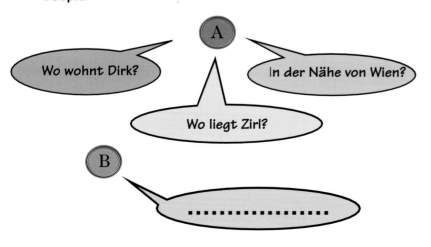

A

Wo wohnt Dirk?

In der Nähe von Wien?

Wo liegt Zirl?

B

....

Tip des Tages

Wo liegt	Rellingen? Erding? Siegburg? Freital? Klausdorf?
Im	Norden. Süden. Osten. Westen. Nordosten. Südosten. Nordwesten. Südwesten.
In der Nähe von	Hamburg. München. Dresden.

sb ▶ *Selbstbedienung*

Lernziel 1

🏳 **Länderquiz**

Welches Land ist das?

Beispiel
1 *Das ist Dänemark.*

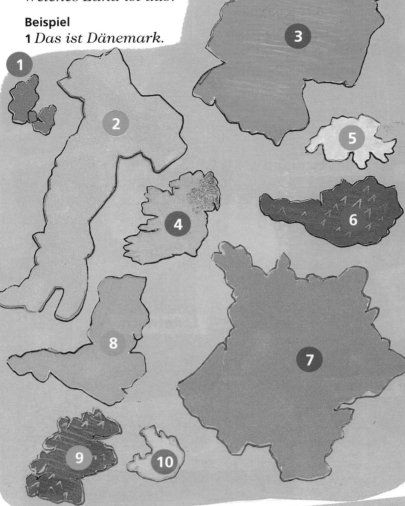

Lernziel 1

🏴 **Die Hauptstadt von Italien ist Rom**

Füll die Lücken aus.

Beispiel
1 *Die Hauptstadt von Italien ist Rom.*

1 Die Hauptstadt von It – – – – – – ist – – m.
2 Die Hauptstadt von S – – – – – – – – – d ist E – – – – – – g.
3 Die Hauptstadt von D – – – – – – land ist – – – – in.
4 Die Hauptstadt von Fr – – – – – – ch ist – – ri –.
5 Die Hauptstadt von der S – – – eiz ist B – – n.

Jetzt kannst du andere Lückensätze schreiben!

Lernziel 2

🏳 **Das Auto kommt aus …**

Beispiel
D = *aus Deutschland*

aus Frankreich	aus der Schweiz
aus Deutschland	aus Österreich
aus Dänemark	aus Luxemburg

Lernziel 2

Purzelwörter

Wie schreibt man das richtig?

Beispiel
1 LUXEMBURG

Länder
1 RUBMEXGLU
2 SICWHEZ
3 LATHCDNUSED
4 BILGNEE
5 SLAWE
6 MÄDKRANE
7 RINKERCHAF

Städte
1 HUGBARM
2 NEWI
3 NLIZ
4 CHÜZRI
5 NERB
6 NONB
7 NELBIR

Lernziel 3

Zahlenrätsel

1 *Sieh dir diese drei Länder an: DEUTSCHLAND, ÖSTERREICH, SCHWEIZ. Welche Buchstaben sind in allen drei Ländern? Schreib sie auf – sie bilden eine Zahl. Welche Zahl ist das?*

2 *Welche Zahl ist im Land SCHWEIZ zu finden?*

3 *Welche Zahl ist im Land DEUTSCHLAND zu finden?*

Kannst du andere Zahlenrätsel mit Ländern schreiben?

Lernziel 3

Alphabeträtsel

Was ist die Frage?

Was ist in …   aber nicht in …

… Wien	… Belgien?
… sieben	… sechs?
… Name	… man?
… aus	… auf?
… sechzehn	… siebzehn?
… ich	… du?
… richtig	… wichtig?
… Anne	… Anna?
… sieh	… stell?
… bist	… ist?
… rot	… gold?
… Mainz	… Linz?
… Tag	… Morgen?
… zehn	… zwei?
… Nord	… Ost?
… zwanzig	… zwölf?
… Susi	… Ulli?

Kannst du andere Alphabeträtsel schreiben?

Lernziel 3

Wo liegt Grasdorf?

Wo liegen die Dörfer?

Beispiel
1 *Grasdorf liegt im Nordosten, in der Nähe von Strandburg.*

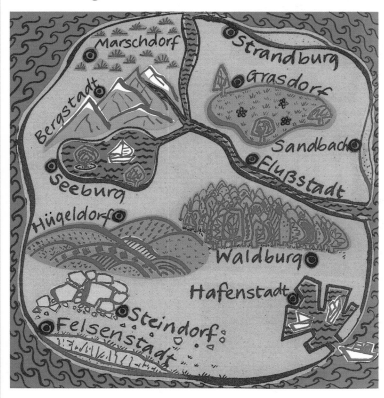

Schau jetzt im Wörterbuch nach — was bedeuten die Namen der Dörfer und Städte?

Zum Lesen

Auch wir sprechen Deutsch!

Wo spricht man Deutsch?
Nicht nur in Deutschland, Österreich, Luxemburg,
Liechtenstein und der Schweiz, sondern auch ... überall!

Hallo! Ich heiße Detlev, und ich wohne in Prag. Ich spreche Deutsch.

CENTRO CITTA' BOLZANO
BOZEN STADTZENTRUM

Ich heiße Laura. Ich komme aus Norditalien, aber Deutsch ist meine Muttersprache. Ich wohne in Bruneck, in der Nähe von Bozen.

Mein Name ist Ralf. Ich komme aus Amerika. Ich wohne in Pennsylvania, in der Nähe von Pittsburgh. Ich bin Mitglied der Amischen Gemeinschaft.

Hallo! Ich heiße Ludmila. Ich wohne in Rußland, aber Deutsch ist meine Muttersprache. Meine Familie wohnt schon lange hier in Rußland.

Guten Tag! Ich bin Bernhardt. Ich wohne in Australien, im Barossa Tal.

1 Asking questions

Woher kommst du?		*Where do you come from?*
Wo wohnst du?		*Where do you live?*

Wo liegt	Hamburg?	Where is	*Hamburg?*	
	München?		*Munich?*	
	Bonn?		*Bonn?*	
	Dresden?		*Dresden?*	

2 Saying where you come from

Ich komme aus	Irland.	I come from	*Ireland.*
	Österreich.		*Austria.*
	der Schweiz.		*Switzerland.*

Ich wohne in	Dublin.	I live in	*Dublin.*
	Wien.		*Vienna.*
	Basel.		*Basle.*

3 Saying where your town is

Das liegt im	Norden.	That's in the	*north.*
	Süden.		*south.*
	Osten.		*east.*
	Westen.		*west.*
	Nordosten.		*northeast.*
	Südosten.		*southeast.*
	Nordwesten.		*northwest.*
	Südwesten.		*southwest.*

In der Nähe von	Manchester.	Near	*Manchester.*
	Cardiff.		*Cardiff.*
	Aberdeen.		*Aberdeen.*

Lernziel 1
Hast du Geschwister?

🎞 **Wie heißen sie?**

Hör gut zu. Worum geht es hier?
Schreib die Namen in der
richtigen Reihenfolge auf.
Beispiel
1 *David*

Ich habe eine
Schwester.

Maren

Ich habe einen
Stiefbruder.

Dorit

Ich habe
einen Bruder und
eine Schwester.

David

Ich habe einen
Bruder und
eine Schwester.

Emine

Ich bin ein Einzelkind.

Raphael

Ich habe
einen Bruder.

Maria

Ich habe zwei Brüder
und eine Schwester.

Peter

Ich habe zwei
Schwestern.

Ute

Ich habe keine
Geschwister.

Ahmed

Ich habe drei Brüder
und zwei Schwestern.

Oliver

Partnerarbeit. Welche Familie ist das?

Hier sind zwölf Familien.
Wähl eine Familie, und beantworte alle Fragen mit ‚Ja' oder ‚Nein'.

Beispiel

A – Ja, fertig.
B – Hast du Brüder?
A – Ja.
B – Hast du einen Bruder?
A – Ja.

B – Hast du Schwestern?
A – Nein.
B – (Also … du hast einen Bruder und keine Schwestern)
– das ist Familie eins.
A – Richtig. Jetzt bist du dran.

Tip des Tages

Hast du Geschwister?			einen Bruder. eine Schwester.
Nein, ich habe keine Geschwister.	Ja, ich habe	zwei drei vier	Brüder.
Ich bin ein Einzelkind.			Schwestern.

Lernziel 2

Das ist meine Familie

🔲 **Mein Stammbaum**

Das ist Jürgens Familie.
Hör gut zu. Wie heißen sie?
Beispiel
Jürgens Bruder heißt Lutz.

mein Cousin

meine Cousine

meine Stiefschwester

meine Tante

Jürgen

Das ist meine Familie.

mein Bruder

mein Onkel

meine Mutter

mein Vater

mein Großvater

meine Großmutter

Kurt	Michael	
Gisela	Nicole	Lutz
Helga	Bernd	
Luise	Paul	Sonja

Partnerarbeit

Du bist Jürgen! Beantworte Fragen über deine Familie.
Beispiel
A – Wie heißt deine Tante?
B – (Sie heißt) Luise.
A – Richtig. Jetzt bist du dran.
B – Wie heißt dein Onkel?
A – (Er heißt) ...

Zwei Briefe

*Lies die Briefe, und sieh dir die Fotos an.
Welches Foto paßt zu welchem Brief.
Vorsicht – ein Foto paßt zu
keinem Brief!*

Wien, den 20. Oktober

Liebe Rachel,
Grüß Dich! Ich wohne in Wien. Das ist die
Hauptstadt von Österreich. Ich bin 13
Jahre alt. Wie alt bist Du?
Ich habe einen Bruder und eine Schwester.
Schreib mir bitte bald!
Herzliche Grüße,
Deine Maria
P.S. Ich lege Dir ein Foto von uns drei bei.

Bonn, den 1. April

Lieber John!
Hallo! Ich wohne in Bonn in Deutschland.
Ich bin vierzehn Jahre alt und habe im April
Geburtstag. Ich habe einen Bruder und eine
Schwester. Hast Du Geschwister? Wie alt bist Du?
Schreib bald!

Viele Grüße,
Dein Peter,

P.S. Ich lege Dir ein Foto von uns drei bei.

Tip des Tages

Das ist	mein	Bruder. Stiefbruder. Vater. Stiefvater. Onkel. Großvater. Cousin.
	meine	Schwester. Stiefschwester. Mutter. Stiefmutter. Tante. Großmutter. Cousine.

Wie heißt	dein	Bruder?
	deine	Schwester?

Mein Bruder Er	heißt	Lutz.
Meine Schwester Sie		Anja.

Steffi

Er ist fantastisch . . . so fit . . . und er ist 15!

Quatsch! Der ist erst 13. Das weiß ich.

Was! Dreizehn? Das Schwein! Ich bringe ihn um!

Lernziel 3

Hast du ein Haustier?

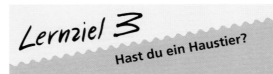 **Ich habe einen Hund**

Hör gut zu, und sieh dir die Fotos an.
Welches Foto paßt?
Beispiel
Christa – 3

Renate?	**Christa?**	**Stefan?**
Martin?	**David?**	**Heike?**

Klaus hat eine Maus

Sieh dir die Tiere an.
Schreib die Sätze auf, und füll die Lücken aus.
Beispiel
1 Klaus hat eine Maus.
2 Gerd hat ein ____ .
3 Frau Bamster hat einen ____ .
4 Herr Lund hat einen ____ .
5 Sabinchen hat zwölf ____ .

Partnerarbeit. Wie heißt der Hund?

Sieh dir die Bilder an. Wie heißen die Tiere?
Stell und beantworte Fragen.
Beispiel
A – Wie heißt der Hund?
B – Schnuffel. Wie heißt die Maus?
A – Fipsi.

Hansi

Rex

Max

Schnuffel

Elsa

Mitzi

Amanda

Fipsi

Stupsi

Tanjas Haustiere

Lies den Brief. Tanja schreibt über ihre Haustiere.

Ich habe sechs Haustiere:

Das ist mein Hamster - er heißt Heinrich.

Das ist mein Hund - er heißt Pino.

Das ist meine Katze - sie heißt Omo.

Das ist meine Maus - sie heißt Mini.

Das ist mein Kaninchen - es heißt Zuckig.

Und das ist mein Pferd - es heißt Jacko.

Jetzt bist du dran!
Beschreib deine Haustiere.

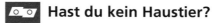 **Hast du kein Haustier?**

Hör gut zu, lies den Text und wiederhol.

Tip des Tages

Hast du ein Haustier?					
Ja, ich habe	einen	Hund. Hamster. Wellensittich.			
	eine	Katze. Maus. Wüstenmaus.			
Klaus hat	ein	Pferd. Kaninchen. Meerschweinchen.			
Nein, ich habe	keinen	Hund.			
	keine	Katze.			
	kein	Haustier.			
Wie heißt	der Hund?	Mein Hund Er		heißt	Schnuffel.
	die Katze?	Meine Katze Sie			Mitzi.
	das Kaninchen?	Mein Kaninchen Es			Stupsi.

sb ▶ Selbstbedienung

Nein. Und du?

Dreizhen. Und du?

Hast du Geschwister?

Ich heiße Jens. Und du?

Wie alt bist du?

Vierzehn.   Christa.

Hallo! Wie heißt du?

In Hamburg. Und wo wohnst du?

Wo wohnst du?

Ich wohne in Bremen.

Ich habe eine Schwester und einen Bruder.

> ## Lernziel 1
>
> ▶ **Und du?**
>
> *Schreib den Dialog in der richtigen Reihenfolge auf.*
> **Beispiel**
> – *Hallo! Wie heißt du?*
> – *Ich heiße Jens. Und du?*

Lernziel 1

 Hallo!

Lies den Brief, und sieh dir die Fotos an.
Wie heißt Uschis Bruder? Und Uschis Schwester?

Berlin, den 7. Oktober

Hallo!
Ich wohne in Berlin. Ich bin zwölf Jahre alt.
Ich habe einen Bruder – er ist sechzehn Jahre
alt, und eine Schwester – sie ist vier Jahre alt.
Schreib bald!
Deine Uschi

Mein Name ist Bernd.
Ich bin sechzehn Jahre
alt.

Ich bin Jutta.
Ich bin vier Jahre alt.

Ich heiße Bettina.
Ich bin sechzehn
Jahre alt.

Hallo! Ich heiße Jens.
Ich bin vier Jahre alt.

Lernziel 3

 Was ist das?

Beispiel
1 *Das ist mein Hund.*

Lernziel 2

 Graf Draculas Familie

Graf Dracula stellt seine Familie vor.
Sieh dir das Bild an, und lies den Text.
Wer ist Nummer 1? Und Nummer 2?
Beispiel
1 *Graf Draculas Katze*

> Hier ist meine Schwester. Sie heißt Trudi.
> Das hier ist meine Katze – Kratzleck.
> Hier ist mein Großvater, Waldemar.
> Das hier ist mein Hund, Griff.
> Das ist mein Bruder: Er heißt Rudi.
> Hier ist meine Fledermaus, Blitz.
> Das ist meine Großmutter, Grusela.

Lernziel 3

 Such die Tiere

Welcher Titel paßt am bestem
zu welchem Text?
Beispiel
1c

a **Igelfamilie zu Gast im Hotel Sonne**

b **Katze frißt Wellensittich!**

c **Ich möchte so gerne einen Hamster**

d **Machen Sie Ferien? Denken Sie auch an Ihre Katze!**

1 EINE 12-JÄHRIGE: Alle meine Freundinnen haben ein Tier, nur ich nicht, und ich möchte so gerne einen Goldhamster haben. Mein Vater sagt, Hamster stinken und sind nicht stubenrein.
Bitte helfen Sie mir, ich möchte so gerne einen Hamster.

2 Seit einer Woche kommt jeden Abend pünktlich um halb sieben eine Igelmutter mit ihren drei Jungen auf die Terrasse des Hotels Sonne, wo ein Teller Milch auf sie wartet.

3 Als die kleine Christa M., 9 Jahre alt, den Trickfilm *Tom und Jerry* sah, fraß ihre Katze den Wellensittich.
Die kleine Christa ist unglücklich ...

4 KATZENHOTEL FRÖHLICH Brokenlande.
20 Autominuten von Hamburg.

Bildvokabeln

Ungewöhnliche Haustiere

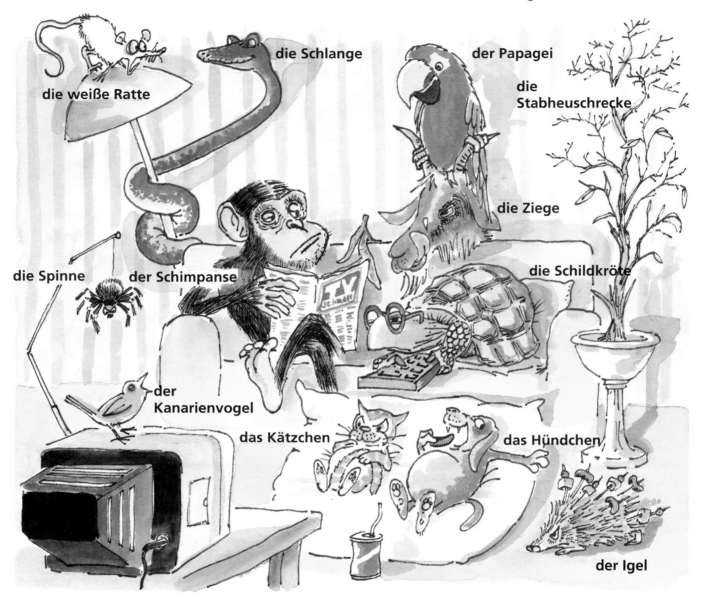

die weiße Ratte

die Schlange

der Papagei

die Stabheuschrecke

die Ziege

die Spinne

der Schimpanse

die Schildkröte

der Kanarienvogel

das Kätzchen

das Hündchen

der Igel

Wie viele Flöhe?

Wie gut bist du in Mathematik?
Lies das Gedicht vor, und beantworte die Frage.

Eine Familie mit vier Kindern
Ging nach Sandbach von Holzkirchen.
Jedes Kind hatte eine Katze.
Jede Katze hatte vier Kätzchen.
Jedes Kätzchen hatte hundert Flöhe.
Wie viele Flöhe gingen nach Holzkirchen?

Schreib a, b, c oder d.
a 25 600?   c 0?
b 1 600?   d 256?

auf einen Blick

1 Asking questions

Hast du Geschwister?		Have you any brothers and sisters?		
Hast du ein Haustier?		Have you got a pet?		
Wie heißt	dein Bruder?	What's	your brother	called?
	deine Schwester?		your sister	
	der Hund?		the dog	
	die Maus?		the mouse	
	das Kaninchen?		the rabbit	

2 Talking about your family

Ich bin ein Einzelkind.			I'm an only child.		
Ich habe		keine Geschwister.	I haven't got any brothers or sisters.		
		einen Bruder.	I've got	a brother.	
		eine Schwester.		a sister.	
		zwei Brüder.		two brothers.	
		drei Schwestern.		three sisters.	
Das ist	mein	Vater.	This is my	father.	
		Onkel.		uncle.	
		(Stief)bruder.		(step)brother.	
		Großvater.		grandfather.	
	meine	Mutter.		mother.	
		Tante.		aunt.	
		(Stief)schwester.		(step)sister.	
		Großmutter.		grandmother.	
Mein Bruder / Er	heißt	Lutz.	My brother / He	is called	Lutz.
Meine Schwester / Sie		Nicole.	My sister / She		Nicole.

3 Talking about your pets

Ich habe / Klaus hat	einen	Hamster.	I've got / Klaus has got	a hamster.
	eine	Katze.		a cat.
	ein	Pferd.		a horse.
Ich habe	keinen	Hund.	I haven't got	a dog.
	keine	Maus.		a mouse.
	kein	Haustier.		any pets.
Das ist	mein Hund.		This is	my dog.
	Er	heißt Schnuffel.		It's called Schnuffel.
Das ist	meine Katze.		This is	my cat.
	Sie	heißt Mitzi.		It's called Mitzi.
Das ist	mein Kaninchen.		This is	my rabbit.
	Es	heißt Stupsi.		It's called Stupsi.

Lernziel 1

Ich wohne in …

Ich wohne am Stadtrand. Wir haben einen Bungalow. Er ist sehr groß.

Frauke

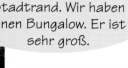

Ich wohne am Stadtrand. Wir haben eine Wohnung. Sie ist ziemlich klein.

Halil

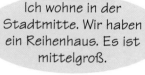

Ich wohne in der Stadtmitte. Wir haben ein Reihenhaus. Es ist mittelgroß.

Sven

 Ich wohne in einem Dorf

Hör zu, und sieh dir die Bilder an. Wer spricht?
Beispiel
1 *Jutta*

Ich wohne in einem Dorf, am Marktplatz. Wir haben ein Einfamilienhaus. Es ist sehr groß.

Dorit

Ich wohne in der Stadtmitte. Wir haben eine Wohnung. Sie ist klein.

Bernd

Ich wohne in einem Dorf. Wir haben ein Haus. Es ist ziemlich groß.

Jutta

Und du? Wo wohnst du?

Tip des Tages

Wo wohnst du?										
Ich wohne	in	einer (Groß)stadt. einem Dorf. der Stadtmitte.	Wir haben	einen	Bungalow.	Er		sehr	groß.
				eine	Wohnung.	Sie	ist	ziemlich	klein.
	am	Stadtrand.		ein	(Einfamilien)haus. Reihenhaus.	Es		mittelgroß.	

Partnerarbeit. Wo denn?

Wähl einen Wohnort, und beantworte alle Fragen mit ‚Ja‘ oder ‚Nein‘.

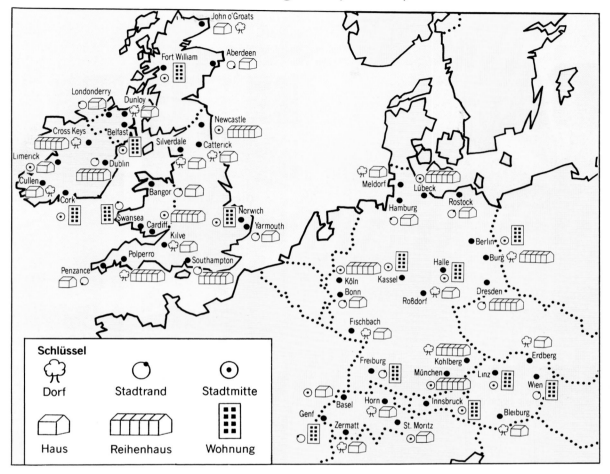

Wohnst du in Deutschland/in der Schweiz/in Österreich/in Schottland/ in Irland/in Nordirland/in Wales/in England?	Ja/Nein
Wohnst du im Norden/im Süden/im Osten/im Westen?	Ja/Nein
Wohnst du in einer Stadt/in einem Dorf?	Ja/Nein
Wohnst du am Stadtrand/in der Stadtmitte?	Ja/Nein
Wohnst du in einem Haus/in einem Reihenhaus/in einer Wohnung? Du wohnst in ...!	Ja/Nein

Beispiel

A – Ja, fertig. Wo wohne ich?
B – Wohnst du in Deutschland?
A – Nein.
B – Wohnst du in der Schweiz?
A – Nein.
B – In England?
A – Ja.
B – Im Norden?

A – Nein
B – Im Süden?
A – Ja.
B – Wohnst du am Stadtrand?
A – Ja.
B – In einem Reihenhaus?
A – Ja.
B – Wohnst du in Southampton?
A – Ja, richtig. Jetzt bist du dran.

Lernziel 2
Die Zimmer

Das ist...
das Wohnzimmer

⬛⬛ **Das ist das Wohnzimmer**

Hör gut zu. Schreib die Zimmer in der richtigen Reihenfolge auf.
Beispiel
2 *(das Wohnzimmer)*

die Küche

das Wohnzimmer

das Badezimmer

mein Zimmer

der Keller

die Toilette

das Eßzimmer

das Zimmer von meiner Schwester

das Zimmer von meinem Bruder

das Schlafzimmer von meinen Eltern

◖◗ **Partnerarbeit. Wie ist dein Haus/deine Wohnung?**

Zeichne einen Plan, und stell Fragen.
Beispiel
A – Das ist mein Haus/meine Wohnung. Was ist das?
B – (Ist das) die Toilette?
A – Nein – das Badezimmer. Was ist das?
B – (Ist das) das Schlafzimmer von deinen Eltern?
A – Nein.
B – (Ist das) dein Zimmer?
A – Nein.
B – (Ist das) das Zimmer von deinem Bruder/deiner Schwester?
A – Ja.

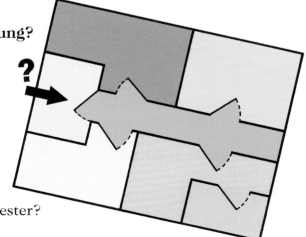

Krabbi

Lies das Gedicht, und hör gut zu.

– Morgen, Krabbi. Was ist los?
– Mein Haus ist zu alt
Und zu kalt und zu groß.
Dein Haus ist viel besser.
Ich möchte so gern
Ein Reihenhaus haben,
So klein und modern.
Sag mal, was für Zimmer
Hat es, dein Haus?
Ich möchte sie sehen.
Komm doch heraus!

Mein Traumhaus

Lies den Text.

Mein Traumhaus: Ein
Haus in Frankreich.
In einem Dorf im Süden.
Sehr groß und alt.
Acht Zimmer.

Mein Traumhaus: Eine
Luxuswohnung in New
York. Sehr groß und
modern mit Balkon.
Sechs Zimmer und
zwei Badezimmer.

Jetzt bist du dran. Beschreib dein Traumhaus.

Zu verkaufen

Sieh dir die Bilder und die Schilder an.
Welches Schild paßt zu welchem Bild?

A
ZU VERKAUFEN
Wohnwagen
Schlaf-/Eß-/Wohn-
/Badezimmer
Sehr kompakt

B
ZU VERKAUFEN
Einfamilienhaus
Fließend
Wasser

C
ZU VERKAUFEN
Schloß
100 Zimmer
Großer Garten

D
ZU VERKAUFEN
Hochhaus mit
Seeblick
Ein Zimmer
Sehr hell

Tip des Tages

Das ist	der Keller. die Küche. das Wohnzimmer. das Badezimmer.		
Hier ist	das Zimmer das Schlafzimmer	von	meinem Bruder. meiner Schwester. meinen Eltern.
	mein Zimmer.		

Was ist dein Traumhaus?		
Ein Haus	im Süden. in Paris.	Mit Balkon. Sehr groß und modern. Sehr alt.
Eine Luxuswohnung	in einem Dorf.	

Lernziel 3
Telefonnummern und Adressen

 Meine Adresse

Hör gut zu. Wer spricht?
Schreib die Namen auf.
Beispiel
1 *Barbara*

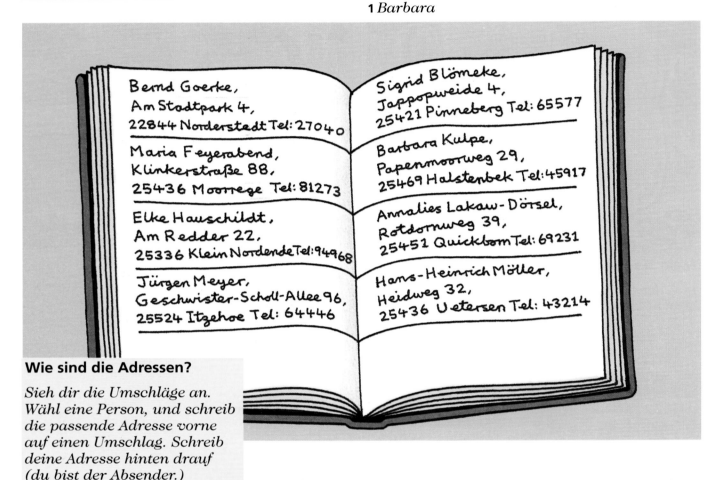

Bernd Goerke,
Am Stadtpark 4,
22844 Norderstedt Tel: 27040

Maria Feyerabend,
Klinkerstraße 88,
25436 Moorrege Tel: 81273

Elke Hauschildt,
Am Redder 22,
25336 Klein Nordende Tel: 94968

Jürgen Meyer,
Geschwister-Scholl-Allee 96,
25524 Itzehoe Tel: 64446

Sigrid Blömeke,
Jappopweide 4,
25421 Pinneberg Tel: 65577

Barbara Kulpe,
Papenmoorweg 29,
25469 Halstenbek Tel: 45917

Annalies Lakaw-Dörsel,
Rotdornweg 39,
25451 Quickborn Tel: 69231

Hans-Heinrich Möller,
Heidweg 32,
25436 Uetersen Tel: 43214

Wie sind die Adressen?

Sieh dir die Umschläge an.
Wähl eine Person, und schreib
die passende Adresse vorne
auf einen Umschlag. Schreib
deine Adresse hinten drauf
(du bist der Absender.)

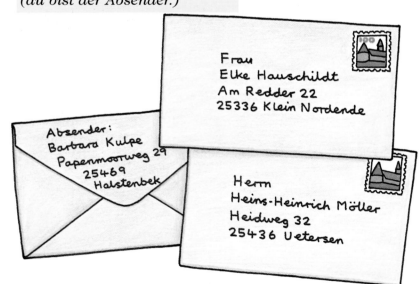

Frau
Elke Hauschildt
Am Redder 22
25336 Klein Nordende

Absender:
Barbara Kulpe
Papenmoorweg 29
25469
Halstenbek

Herrn
Heins-Heinrich Möller
Heidweg 32
25436 Uetersen

Partnerarbeit. Wer bin ich?

Wähl eine Telefonnummer – dein(e)
Partner(in) auch.
Stell und beantworte die Frage und
finde heraus, wer dein(e) Partner(in)
ist! Du hast nur zehn Sekunden.
Beispiel
A – Wie ist deine Telefonnummer?
B – Vier-fünf-neun-eins-sieben.
         Und deine Telefonnummer?
A – Zwei-sieben-null-vier-null.

A – Du bist Barbara!
B – Du bist Bernd!

Computerliste

Elsa ist Computerfan und hat einen neuen Computer.
Hier ist die Computerliste von Elsas Freunden.
Sie tippt aber nicht so gut!
Hör gut zu. Kannst du die drei Tippfehler finden?

Programm: ELSAFREUND

1   Vorname: Anna
     Familienname: Braun
     Adresse: Krokusweg 27, 33335 Gütersloh
     Telefonnummer: 4403

2   Vorname: Peter
     Familienname: Schultz
     Adresse: Feldstraße 1, 25462 Rellingen
     Telefonnummer: 4888

3   Vorname: Klaus
     Familienname: Schmaus
     Adresse: Poststraße 22, 25361 Krempe
     Telefonnummer: 4816

4   Vorname: Barbara
     Familienname: Müller
     Adresse: Hauptstraße 85, 22845 Norderstedt
     Telefonnummer: 4998

5   Vorname: Monika
     Familienname: Schätzle
     Adresse: Zum Sportplatz 7, 25474 Ellerbek
     Telefonnummer: 33201

6   Vorname:
     Familienname:
     Adresse:
     Telefonnummer:

Alter Mann

Hör zu und sing mit.

In der Stadtmitte steht ein alter Mann,
Sechzig oder siebzig Jahre alt.
Keine Adresse, er steht, wo er kann,
Im Winter auf der Straße ist es kalt.

Und niemand weiß,
Wie der Alte heißt,
Das ist eine Frage, die niemand stellt.
Hat er Geschwister?
Hat er einen Freund?
Ist er ganz alleine auf der Welt?

In der Stadtmitte steht ein alter Mann
Alte Schuhe und ein alter Hut.
Keine Adresse, er wohnt, wo er kann,
Doch im Sommer ist das Wetter gut.

Und niemand weiß,
Wie der Alte heißt,
Das ist eine Frage, die niemand stellt.
Hat er Geschwister?
Hat er einen Freund?
Ist er ganz alleine auf der Welt?

In der Stadtmitte steht ein alter Mann.
Er ist nicht mehr so aufrecht, wie er war.
Keine Adresse, er schläft, wo er kann.
Eines Tages ist er nicht mehr da.

Und niemand weiß,
Wie der Alte heißt,
Das ist eine Frage, die niemand stellt.
Hat er Geschwister?
Hat er einen Freund?
Ist er ganz alleine auf der Welt?

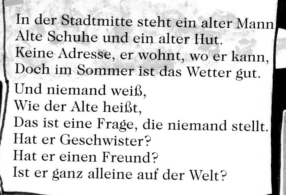

Tip des Tages

Die Zahlen von 21 bis 100

21	einundzwanzig	50	fünfzig
22	zweiundzwanzig	60	sechzig
23	dreiundzwanzig	70	siebzig
30	dreißig	80	achtzig
31	einunddreißig	90	neunzig
40	vierzig	100	hundert

Wie ist deine Adresse?	
Meine Adresse ist	Poststraße 4. Am Stadtpark 16.

Wie ist deine Telefonnummer?	
Meine Telefonnummer ist	vier-sechs-null-zwei-fünf. 4 6 0 2 5. vier-sechzig-fünfundzwanzig.

sb *Selbstbedienung*

Lernziel 1

🚩 **Meine Familie**

Lies den Brief, und sieh dir die Symbole an.
Wo wohnt Annes Familie?

Beispiel
1 = *Anne und ihre Mutter*

Ulm, den 6.Oktober

Lieber Florian,

Hallo! Wie geht's? Heute schreibe ich über meine Familie. Du weißt ja schon, ich wohne in Ulm bei meiner Mutter. Wir haben ein Haus in der Stadtmitte. Mein Vater wohnt auch in Ulm — er hat eine Wohnung am Stadtrand. Ich habe zwei Schwestern. Die eine heißt Ulrike und wohnt in Rellingen. Sie hat ein Reihenhaus am Marktplatz. Meine andere Schwester heißt Sonja. Sie ist 22 und wohnt in Gauting. Das ist ein Dorf in der Nähe von München. Sie hat auch ein Reihenhaus. Mein Großvater und meine Großmutter wohnen in Stuttgart. Sie haben eine kleine Wohnung im Stadtzentrum.
Wie ist Dein Haus? Schreib bald.
Viele Grüße,
Deine Anne

Schlüssel
- Wohnung
- Haus
- Reihenhaus
- Stadtmitte
- Stadtrand
- Dorf
- Marktplatz

Lernziel 2

🚩 **Der Immobilienmarkt**

Was ist das beste Haus oder die beste Wohnung für diese Personen?

Beispiel **A8**

A Wir suchen einen Bungalow in Frankreich oder Spanien.

B Ich suche eine Einzimmerwohnung mit Küche und Badezimmer. Nicht groß, nur dreißig Quadratmeter.

C Wir suchen ein Reihenhaus am Stadtrand mit vier Schlafzimmern.

D Wir suchen eine modernisierte Altbauwohnung mit Schlafzimmer, Wohnzimmer, Küche und Bad.

E Ich suche eine Luxuswohnung in Wiesbaden.

F Wir suchen eine Wohnung mit Balkon und zwei Schlafzimmern.

Der Immobilienmarkt

1 Eppstein-Bremmthal, Luxuswohnung, super Wohnlage, Balkon, 23m², Bad und Gäste-WC, Wohnzimmer, Eßzimmer, Bad, 2 Schlafzimmer B. STAUDT, Südhang 22, 82418 Hofheim

2 Komfort-Reihenhaus, Bj. 1990, Stadtrandlage. 180m² Wohnfläche. Kü., Bad, Wz., Eßzi., 4 Schlfz. Verkaufsbüro Hochheim Tel: 06128/44067

3 Studentenwohnung, 1 Zi., Kü., Bad, 30m² Tel: 0211/591023

4 2-Zi-Wohng., 1993 total modernisiert, Kü., Bad, Wohn- und Schlafzimmer Tel: 0261/782651

5 Penthouse, Kleistraße 11. Die VIP Adresse in Wiesbaden. 3 Zi., Kü., Bad Tel: 06198/841783

6 Doppelhaus: 5 Zi., Einbauküche, Bad/Dusche/WC, Balkon Tel: 06121/522160

7 2-Familienhaus, 5 Zimmer, Küche, Bad, Gäste-WC., Wfl. 145m², Baujahr: 1984 Tel: 06128/41097

8 SPANIEN: COSTA BLANCA Freistehender Bungalow mit Terrasse, Wz., 2 Schlafzimmer, Küche, Bad. 900m² Grundstück. Tel: 07225/34967

Lernziel 2

Welches Zimmer ist das?

Schreib die Namen auf.
Beispiel
1 *die Küche*

Lernziel 3

Wie bitte?

Diese Fragen und Antworten sind durcheinander. Schreib sie in der richtigen Reihenfolge auf.

Wo wohnst du?
Wie ist dein Haus?
Ziemlich klein.
Wie heißt du?
Nein – in der Stadtmitte.
Wohnst du in einem Reihenhaus?
In einem Dorf am Marktplatz.
Wohnst du am Stadtrand?
Mein Schlafzimmer
Leipziger Straße 19.
Wie alt bist du?
Was ist das?
Martina Feyerabend.
Wie ist deine Telefonnummer?
Sieben-null-acht-drei-fünf.
Siebzehn.
Wie ist deine Adresse?
Nein, wir haben eine Wohnung.

Kannst du andere Fragen stellen?

Lernziel 3

Komm zu uns!

Lies die Briefe und beantworte die Fragen.

Freiburg, den 22. Februar
Hallo Derek!
Du lernst Deutsch in der Schule! Toll! Wann kommst Du nach Deutschland? Du kannst zu uns kommen. Wir haben eine Wohnung in der Stadtmitte. Die Wohnung ist groß, und ich habe mein eigenes Zimmer. Du kannst mein Bett haben, und ich schlafe auf der Couch! Wann kommst du? Ich hoffe bald.
Herzliche Grüße,
Dein Werner

Appen, den 2. Januar
Liebe Linda!
Du lernst jetzt Deutsch? Klasse! Kannst Du Ende April nach Appen kommen? Das Wetter ist normalerweise gut zu Ostern. Wir haben ein Haus in Appen. Das ist ein Dorf in Norddeutschland. Das Haus steht am Marktplatz. Es ist sehr groß und alt. Wir haben eine Küche, ein Esszimmer, ein Wohnzimmer und vier Schlafzimmer. Ich habe mein eigenes Zimmer. Es hat ein Bett und eine Couch. Du kannst das Bett haben! Meine Katze Mitzi schläft in der Ecke. Hoffentlich kommst Du Ende April!
Herzliche Grüße,
Deine Bettina

Fragen

1 Wer hat eine Wohnung – Bettina oder Werner?
2 Wer hat ein Haus in Norddeutschland – Bettina oder Werner?
3 Wer hat eine Katze – Bettina oder Werner?
4 Ist Bettinas Haus alt und klein oder groß und alt?
5 Ist Werners Wohnung klein oder groß?
6 Derek ist in Deutschland. Wo schläft Werner – im Bett oder auf der Couch?
7 Linda ist in Deutschland. Wo schläft Bettina – auf der Couch oder im Bett?

Schreib einen Brief an einen Freund/eine Freundin in Deutschland.
Beschreib dein Haus oder deine Wohnung.

Bildvokabeln

Im Haus

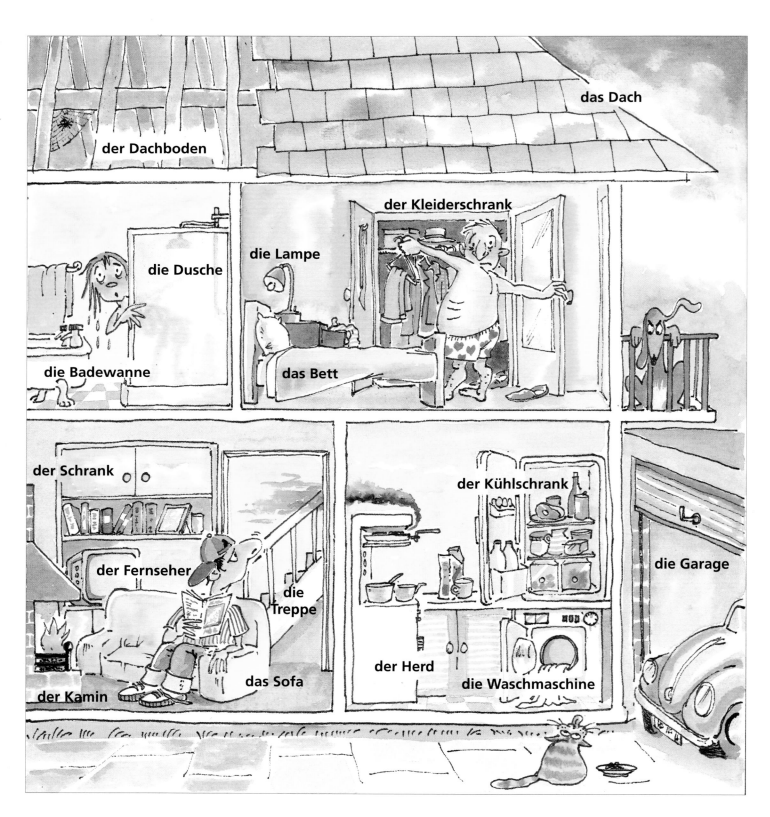

das Dach

der Dachboden

der Kleiderschrank

die Dusche

die Lampe

die Badewanne

das Bett

der Schrank

der Kühlschrank

der Fernseher

die Garage

die Treppe

der Herd

das Sofa

der Kamin

die Waschmaschine

auf einen Blick

1 Asking questions

Wo wohnst du?	*Where do you live?*
Was ist dein Traumhaus?	*What is your dream house?*
Was ist das?	*What is that?*
Wie ist deine Adresse?	*What is your address?*
Wie ist deine Telefonnummer?	*What is your telephone number?*

2 Describing where you live

Ich wohne	in	einer (Groß)stadt. einem Dorf. der Stadtmitte.	*I live*	*in*	*a city/town. a village. the town centre.*
	am	Stadtrand.		*on*	*the outskirts of town.*
Wir haben	einen	Bungalow.	*We have*		*a bungalow.*
	eine	Wohnung.			*a flat.*
	ein	(Einfamilien)haus. Reihenhaus.			*a (detached) house. a terraced house.*
Er Sie Es	ist	sehr groß. ziemlich klein. mittelgroß.	*It is*	*very quite*	*big. small. average sized.*

3 Showing someone around your house or flat

Das ist	der Keller. die Küche. das Wohnzimmer. das Badezimmer.		*This is*	*the cellar. the kitchen. the living room. the bathroom.*
Hier ist	das Zimmer	von	meinem Bruder. meiner Schwester.	*Here is*	*my brother's room. my sister's room.*
	das Schlafzimmer		meinen Eltern.		*my parents' bedroom.*
	mein Zimmer.				*my room.*

4 Talking about your dream house/flat

Ein Haus Eine Luxuswohnung	im Süden. in Paris. in einem Dorf.	*A house A luxury appartment*	*in the south. in Paris. in a village.*
Mit Balkon. Sehr groß und modern. Sehr alt.		*With a balcony. Very large and modern. Very old.*	

5 Numbers from 21 to 100

21 einundzwanzig	30 dreißig	40 vierzig	70 siebzig	100 hundert
22 zweiundzwanzig	31 einunddreißig	50 fünfzig	80 achtzig	
23 dreiundzwanzig		60 sechzig	90 neunzig	

6 Giving your address and telephone number

Meine Adresse ist	Poststraße 4. Am Stadtpark 16.	*My address is*	*Poststraße 4. Am Stadtpark 16.*
Meine Telefonnummer ist	vier-sechs-null-zwei-fünf. vier-sechzig-fünfundzwanzig.	*My telephone number is 4 60 25.*	

Lernziel 1

Wie spät ist es?

Hör gut zu. Wie spät ist es?

Beispiel
1 *Es ist ein Uhr.*

●● **Partnerarbeit. Zeig auf die Uhr**

1 fünf nach zwei

2 zehn nach zwei

3 Viertel nach zwei

4 fünfundzwanzig nach zwei

5 halb drei

6 zwanzig vor drei

7 Viertel vor drei

8 fünf vor drei

Beispiel
A – Es ist Viertel nach zwei. Zeig auf die Uhr.

B – Hier, Nummer 3.
A – Richtig. Jetzt bist du dran.

Entschuldigung. Wieviel Uhr ist es?

Hör gut zu. Wieviel Uhr ist es?

Beispiel
1 G (9.30)

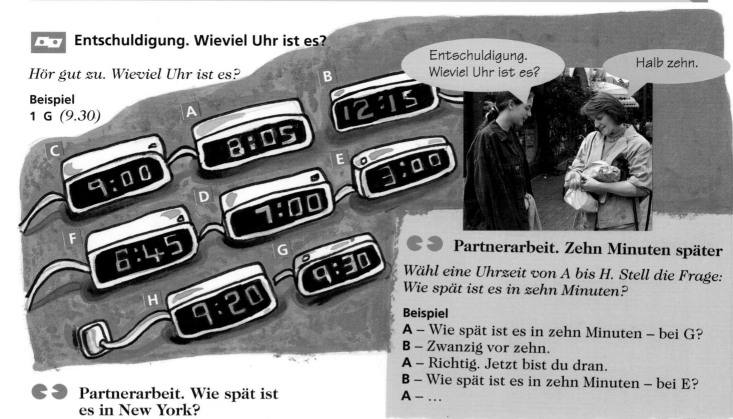

> Entschuldigung. Wieviel Uhr ist es?

> Halb zehn.

Partnerarbeit. Zehn Minuten später

Wähl eine Uhrzeit von A bis H. Stell die Frage: Wie spät ist es in zehn Minuten?

Beispiel
A – Wie spät ist es in zehn Minuten – bei G?
B – Zwanzig vor zehn.
A – Richtig. Jetzt bist du dran.
B – Wie spät ist es in zehn Minuten – bei E?
A – …

Partnerarbeit. Wie spät ist es in New York?

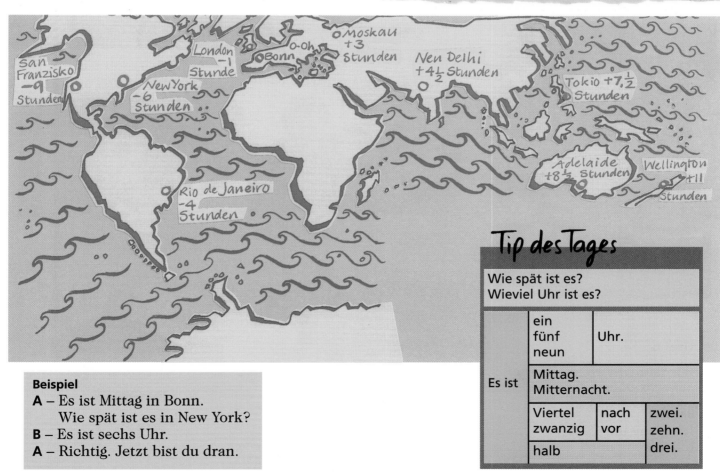

Beispiel
A – Es ist Mittag in Bonn.
  Wie spät ist es in New York?
B – Es ist sechs Uhr.
A – Richtig. Jetzt bist du dran.

Tip des Tages

Wie spät ist es?
Wieviel Uhr ist es?

	ein fünf neun	Uhr.	
Es ist	Mittag. Mitternacht.		
	Viertel zwanzig	nach vor	zwei. zehn.
	halb		drei.

Lernziel 2

Tagesroutine

Martina beschreibt ihren Alltag

Hör gut zu.
Was macht Martina? Um wieviel Uhr?

Beispiel
1 *Um 6 Uhr*

1   Ich stehe auf.

2   Ich wasche mich.

3   Ich frühstücke.

4   Ich verlasse das Haus.

5   Der Unterricht beginnt.

6   Die Schule ist aus.

7   Ich esse mein Mittagessen.

8   Ich mache meine Hausaufgaben.

9   Ich treffe mich mit Freunde

10   Ich sehe fern.

11   Ich esse mein Abendbrot.

12   Ich gehe ins Bett.

Und du?

Wie ist deine Tagesroutine?
Schreib sie auf.

Beispiel
Ich stehe um … auf.
Ich wasche mich …

Katzenalltag

Lies das Gedicht.

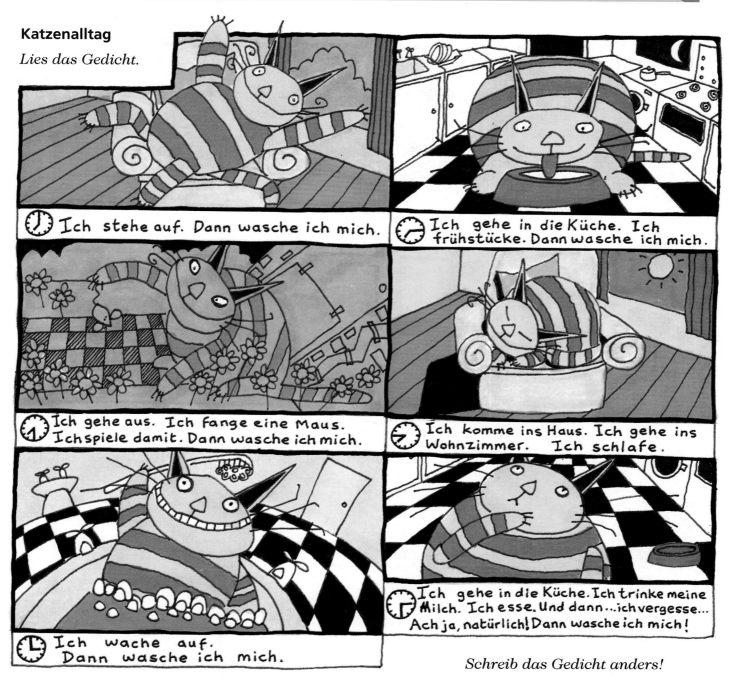

Ich stehe auf. Dann wasche ich mich.

Ich gehe in die Küche. Ich frühstücke. Dann wasche ich mich.

Ich gehe aus. Ich fange eine Maus. Ich spiele damit. Dann wasche ich mich.

Ich komme ins Haus. Ich gehe ins Wohnzimmer. Ich schlafe.

Ich wache auf. Dann wasche ich mich.

Ich gehe in die Küche. Ich trinke meine Milch. Ich esse. Und dann...ich vergesse... Ach ja, natürlich! Dann wasche ich mich!

Schreib das Gedicht anders!

Tip des Tages

Ich	stehe	um sechs Uhr auf.
Ich	wasche	mich um Viertel nach sechs.
Der Unterricht	beginnt	um halb acht.
Die Schule	ist	um ein Uhr aus.
Um Viertel vor zwei	esse	ich.
Ich	gehe	um halb zehn ins Bett.

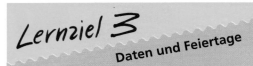

Lernziel 3
Daten und Feiertage

Geburtstagsumfrage

Wann haben die meisten Schüler aus der siebten Klasse in der Realschule in Rellingen Geburtstag?

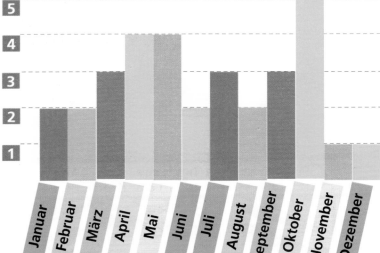

Wann hast du Geburtstag?

Hör gut zu.
Wann haben die zehn Teenager Geburtstag?

Beispiel
Sonja – am 3. August

> Am dritten August. Und du?

> Wann hast du Geburtstag?

Partnerarbeit

A – Wieviel Schüler haben im Januar Geburtstag?
B – Zwei. Wieviel Schüler haben im ... Geburtstag?

Ein Geburtstag in der Familie

Hör gut zu.
Wer hat den ersten Geburtstag? Wann?
Wer hat den zweiten?
Schreib die richtige Reihenfolge auf.

Herr Bromma
Maria
Frau Bromma
Steffi
Lutz

Beispiel
Lutz – am 2. März

Tip des Tages

Wann hast du Geburtstag?			
(Ich habe) am	ersten (1.) zweiten (2.) dritten (3.) vierten (4.) sechsten (6.) siebten (7.) elften (11.) neunzehnten (19.) zwanzigsten (20.) fünfundzwanzigsten (25.) dreißigsten (30.) einunddreißigsten (31.)	Januar Februar März April Mai Juni Juli August September Oktober November Dezember	(Geburtstag).

Wann sind die Feiertage?

Lies den Text und sieh dir die Bilder an. Welches Datum paßt?

Beispiel *Valentinstag – am vierzehnten Februar*

im Mai
am fünfundzwanzigsten Dezember
Ende März/Anfang April
Ende Februar/Anfang März
am vierzehnten Februar
am einunddreißigsten Dezember
am ersten Januar
Ende Oktober
Ende Januar/Anfang Februar
im Dezember

Das Fest von Christi Auferstehung. Zum Osterfest bringt der Osterhase bunt gefärbte Ostereier.

An diesem Tag schicken sich Liebhaber Karten – aber anonym.

Das größte christliche Fest des Jahres – man bekommt Weihnachtsgeschenke und singt Weihnachtslieder, um die Geburt Christi zu feiern.

Dieses jüdische Lichtfest dauert acht Tage. Man zündet Kerzen auf der Menora an und schenkt sich Geschenke. Die Kinder machen Spiele.

Die Jahreswende – der Beginn eines neuen Jahres.

Der letzte Tag des Jahres, nach Papst Silvester (geb. 314 – gest. 335).

Das heilige Fastmonat nach dem mohammedanischen Kalender.

An diesem Tag hat Gott den heiligen Geist auf die Erde geschickt.

Dieses Fest dauert einen Monat. Es gibt Straßentheaterstücke und Feierzüge, um böse Geister auszutreiben.

Das hinduistische Lichtfest. Am vierten Tag des Festes beginnt das neue Jahr.

Kannst du deinen eigenen Bildkalender malen?

Steh auf!

Hör zu und sing mit.

1
Guten Morgen! Guten Morgen!
Steh auf! Steh auf!
Noch nicht! Noch nicht!
Ich bin müde! Ich bin müde!

2
Halb sieben! Halb sieben!
Mach schnell! Mach schnell!
Ach nein! Ach nein!
Ich bin müde! Ich bin müde!

3
Und die Schule? Und die Schule?
Halb acht! Halb acht!
Ich weiß! Ich weiß!
Ich bin müde! Ich bin müde!

4
Acht Uhr zwanzig! Acht Uhr zwanzig!
Zu spät! Zu spät!
Gut' Nacht! Gut' Nacht!
Ich bin müde! Ich bin müde!

sb ▶ Selbstbedienung

Lernziel 1

🏳️ **Wieviel Uhr ist es?**

Wähl die passenden Uhrzeiten, und schreib sie auf.

Beispiel
1 *Es ist fünfundzwanzig nach elf.*

Es ist | Mittag.
fünfundzwanzig nach elf.
Viertel nach acht.
zwanzig vor zehn.
Viertel vor neun.
halb sieben.

Lernziel 1

🏴 **Wo sind sie?**

Wo sind diese Leute?
Sieh dir die Bilder, die Uhrzeiten
und die Weltkarte (Seite 47) an.

Beispiel
1 *New York*

Es ist 2.00 Uhr
nachmittags in
Deutschland.
Eric ist in ...?

Es ist Mittag in
Deutschland.
Olga ist in ...?

Es ist 9.00 Uhr
vormittags in
Deutschland.
Maria ist in ...?

Es ist Mitternacht
in Deutschland.
Peter ist in ...?

Es ist 13.30 Uhr
nachmittags in
Deutschland.
Youhei ist in ...?

Es ist Mitternacht
in Deutschland.
Sandy ist in ...?

Lernziel 2

🏳️ **Füll die Lücken aus.**

Beispiel
1 *Ich stehe um 7 Uhr auf.*

Ich ____ um 7 Uhr auf.

Dann ____ ich um ____ ____.

____ verlasse das ____
um ____ ____ ____.

Die Schule ist um
____ ____ ____ aus.

____ ____ nach ____
sehe ich ____.

Ich gehe ____ ____
____ ins ____.

Lernziel 2

🏴 Evi Bamms Tagesroutine

*Sieh dir die Bilder und Texte an,
und beschreib Evi Bamms Tagesroutine.*
Wähl den richtigen Satz.
Füll die Lücken aus.

Beispiel

A *Sie steht um elf Uhr morgens auf.*
Um _____ geht sie in die Disco.
Sie steht um _____ _____ morgens auf.
Sie geht um _____ _____ ins Bett.
_____ _____ _____ _____ frühstückt sie.
_____ _____ Uhr arbeitet sie.
Um _____ _____ geht sie in die Stadt.

Lernziel 3

🏴 Wann denn?

*Schreib die Daten und
Uhrzeiten der Popkonzerte auf.*

Beispiel

1 *Evi Bamm – am Sonntag,
dem vierzehnten November,
um acht Uhr abends.*

Lernziel 3

🏴 Was fehlt?

*Schreib folgende Sätze auf,
und füll die Lücken aus.*

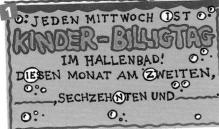

Zum Lesen

Was machst du an deinem Geburtstag?

Tina
Ich gehe in die Stadt.

1

2

Kirsten
Ich gebe eine Party.

3

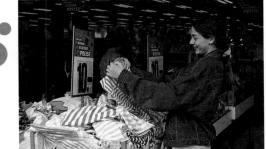

Jens
Ich treffe mich
mit Freunden.

4

Thomas
Wir gehen ins Kino.

Markus
Ich gehe
ins Restaurant.

5

6

Nina
Nichts Besonderes.

Und du?

Was machst du an deinem Geburtstag?
Bist du wie Tina? Oder Jens? Oder Nina?

Tip des Tages

Was machst du an deinem Geburtstag?	
Nichts Besonderes.	
Ich	gehe in die Stadt. gehe ins Kino. gebe eine Party. treffe mich mit Freunden. gehe ins Restaurant.

1 Asking questions

Wie spät Wieviel Uhr	ist es?	What time is it?
Wann hast du Geburtstag?		When is your birthday?
Was machst du an deinem Geburtstag?		What do you do on your birthday?

2 Telling the time

Es ist	ein fünf neun	Uhr.		It is	one five nine	o'clock.	
	Mittag. Mitternacht.				midday. midnight.		
	Viertel zwanzig	nach vor	zwei. zehn.		a quarter twenty	past to	two. ten.
	halb		drei.		half past		two.

3 Giving the date

Am	ersten (1.) zweiten (2.) dritten (3.) vierten (4.) sechsten (6.) siebten (7.) elften (11.) neunzehnten (19.) zwanzigsten (20.) fünfundzwanzigsten (25.) dreißigsten (30.) einunddreißigsten (31.)	Januar Februar März April Mai Juni Juli August September Oktober November Dezember	On the	first second third fourth sixth seventh eleventh nineteenth twentieth twenty-fifth thirtieth thirty-first	of	January February March April May June July August September October November December
Ich habe am neunten Mai Geburtstag.			My birthday is on the ninth of May.			

4 Talking about your daily routine

Ich stehe um sieben Uhr auf.	I get up at seven o'clock.
Ich wasche mich um Viertel nach sieben.	I wash at quarter past seven.
Dann frühstücke ich um halb acht.	Then I have breakfast at half past seven.
Ich verlasse das Haus um zehn nach acht.	I leave home at ten past eight.
Der Unterricht beginnt um Viertel vor neun.	Lessons start at a quarter to nine.
Die Schule ist um zwanzig vor vier aus.	School ends at twenty to four.
Nachmittags mache ich meine Hausaufgaben.	I do my homework in the afternoon.
Ich esse mein Abendbrot um halb sieben.	I eat my evening meal at half past six.
Dann treffe ich mich um sieben Uhr mit Freunden.	Then I meet some friends at seven o'clock.
Um acht Uhr sehe ich fern.	I watch TV at eight o'clock.
Dann gehe ich um neun Uhr ins Bett.	Then I go to bed at nine o'clock.

5 Saying what you do on your birthday

Ich gehe in die Stadt.	I go into town.	Wir gehen ins Kino.	We go to the cinema.
Ich gebe eine Party.	I have a party.	Ich gehe ins Restaurant.	I go to a restaurant.
Ich treffe mich mit Freunden.	I meet some friends.	Nichts Besonderes.	Nothing special.

auf einen Blick

6 Wie schmeckt's?

Lernziel 1

Was ißt du zum Frühstück?

Die Frühstückspalette

Sieh dir die Frühstückspalette an, und hör gut zu.
Wer ißt und trinkt was zum Frühstück?
Beispiel

	ißt	**trinkt**
Silvia:	D – Cornflakes mit Milch	F – Kaffee mit Milch

Das Frühstück bei der Familie Braun

Sieh dir die Fotos an, und hör gut zu.
Was ißt jede Person zum Frühstück?
Was trinkt jede Person?
Beispiel
Renate – Brot mit Honig; Milch

Partnerarbeit

Wähl ein Frühstück, und beantworte die Fragen mit ‚ja'
oder ‚nein'.
Beispiel
A – Ja, fertig.
B – Ißt du Brot mit Marmelade?
A – Nein.
B – Ißt du Cornflakes mit Milch?
A – Ja.
B – Trinkst du …?
A – …

Eine Umfrage in einer Schule in Hamburg

Wir haben die Fragen gestellt: ‚Was ißt du zum Frühstück?'
und: ‚Was trinkst du zum Frühstück?'
Hier sind die Antworten von 26 Schülern aus der Klasse 6c:

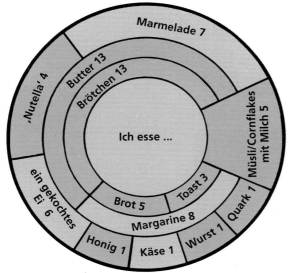

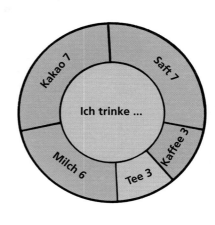

Statistik

1
Wieviel Schüler essen:
a ein gekochtes Ei
b Brötchen
c Wurst
d Honig
e Nutella?

2
Was essen sie?
a Sieben Schüler essen ...
b Sechs Schüler essen ...
c Acht Schüler essen ...
d Dreizehn Schüler essen ...
e Ein Schüler ißt ...

3
Lückentext: Wer trinkt was?
a S___ Schüler trinken K___.
b S___ Schüler ____ M___.
c S___ ____ ____ ____.
d D___ ____ ____ K___.
e ____ ____ ____ ____.

Frühstücksgedicht

Tip des Tages

Was ißt du zum Frühstück?			
	Müsli.		
Ich esse	Brot Brötchen Toast	mit	Butter. Margarine. Honig. Marmelade. Käse. Wurst.
	ein gekochtes Ei. gar nichts.		

Was trinkst du?			
Ich trinke	Tee Kaffee	mit ohne	Milch. Zucker.
	Kakao. Milch. Saft.		

Lernziel 2
Mittagessen und Abendessen

Sonja

Ich esse gern Gulasch mit Nudeln, und ich trinke gern Milch oder Limonade.

A

Was ißt du gern zum Mittagessen?

Hör zu, und sieh dir die Texte und Fotos an. Wer ißt was?

Dorit

Ich esse gern Hähnchen mit Pommes frites, und ich trinke gern Cola oder Saft.

Ich esse gern Frikadellen mit Bratkartoffeln, und ich trinke nichts.

Dieter

B

C

Partnerarbeit. Und du?

Was ißt du gern zum Mittagessen?
Und was trinkst du gern?
Mach Dialoge.

Beispiel

A – Was ißt du gern zum Mittagessen?
B – Frikadellen mit Pommes frites. Und du?
A – Hähnchen mit Bratkartoffeln. Was trinkst du gern?
B – Cola oder Milch. Und du?
A – Kaffee.

Kantine Wochenplan

Sieh dir die Speisekarte an, und beantworte die Fragen.

KANTINE WOCHENPLAN		
MONTAG	1. Bratwurst mit gem. Salatteller und Pommes frites	DM 7,50
	2. Frikadellen mit Röstzwiebeln	DM 5,50
DIENSTAG	1. Spaghetti ‚Bolognese' mit Parmesan-Käse überbacken	DM 7,60
	2. Gulasch mit Nudeln (mit gemischtem Salat)	DM 7,80
MITTWOCH	1. Gegrillter Fisch mit Salzkartoffeln	DM 6,80
	2. Steak auf Toast mit gem. Salatteller	DM 9,50
DONNERSTAG	1. Bockwurst auf Curryreis mit Salat	DM 9,00
	2. Hamburger mit Pommes frites	DM 7,80
FREITAG	1. Hähnchen mit Salat und Bratkartoffeln	DM 8,50
	2. Seelachs-Filet mit Röstkartoffeln	DM 8,00

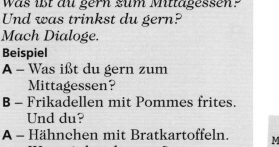

1 Wann gibt es ?

2 Wann gibt es ?

3 Wann gibt es ?

4 Wann gibt es ?

5 Wann gibt es ?

Beispiel 1 *Am Mittwoch und am Freitag*

Das Abendessen. Ein Interview mit der Klasse 6c

Wir haben der Klasse 6c auch diese Fragen gestellt: ‚Was ißt du gern zum Abendessen?' ‚Was trinkst du gern?'
Hier sind die Resultate:

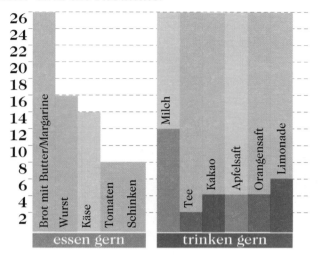

In der Pizzeria

Hör zu, und sieh dir die Speisekarte an.
Was bestellen diese Personen in der Pizzeria?

Jutta: Ich esse nicht gern Salami, Pilze oder Peperoni.
Sabine: Ich esse auch nicht gern Salami, aber ich esse sehr gern Pilze und Paprika.
Frau Bromma: Ich esse gern Oliven und Knoblauch.
Herr Bromma: Ich esse gern Schinken und Pilze.

Jutta bestellt ...
Sabine bestellt ...
Frau Bromma bestellt ...
Herr Bromma bestellt ...
Die Lösung ist auch auf Kassette!

Partnerarbeit

Mach Dialoge mit deinem Partner/deiner Partnerin.
A – Wieviel Schüler in der Klasse essen Brot mit Butter oder Margarine?
B – Sechsundzwanzig. Wieviel trinken Milch?
A – Zwölf.

PIZZA-SPEZIALITÄTEN

PIZZA „PICCOLO" Tomaten, Käse, Salami, Pilze, Paprika	9.80
PIZZA „MARGHERITA" Tomaten, Käse	10.50
PIZZA „SALAMI" Tomaten, Käse, Salami	11.50
PIZZA „PILZE" Tomaten, Käse, Pilze	11.50
PIZZA „SALAMI u. PILZE" Tomaten, Käse, Salami, Pilze	12.00
PIZZA „NAPOLI" Tomaten, Käse, Salami, Schinken, Peperoni	12.50
PIZZA „PEPERONI" Tomaten, Käse, Peperoni, Paprika	12.50
PIZZA „SCHINKEN" Tomaten, Käse, Schinken, Pilze	12.50
PIZZA „MEERESFRÜCHTE" Tomaten, Käse, Meeresfrüchte	13.50
PIZZA „SPEZIAL" Tomaten, Käse, Pilze, Paprika, Sardellen, Oliven, Knoblauch	13.50

Auf Wunsch belegen wir Ihre Pizza mit Zwiebeln.
Mehrpreis DM 2.00

Und du?

Was ißt du gern? Was bestellst du?
Frag auch deinen Partner/deine Partnerin.
Kannst du deine eigene Pizza backen?
Wähl die Zutaten, und zeichne die Pizza.

Tip des Tages

Was ißt du gern zum	Mittagessen? Abendessen?			Was trinkst du gern?	
(Ich esse gern)	Hähnchen Frikadellen Gulasch	mit	Nudeln. Pommes (frites). Bratkartoffeln.	(Ich trinke gern)	Cola. Limonade. Saft. Tee. Kaffee. Milch.
	Brot		Butter/Margarine. Wurst/Käse/Salami/Tomaten/Schinken.		

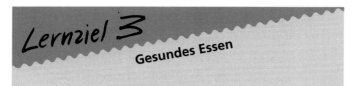

Lernziel 3
Gesundes Essen

 Was heißt ‚gesund essen'?

Diese Teenager sprechen über das Thema ‚gesund essen'.
Hör gut zu, und sieh dir die Bilder und Texte an.
Welches Bild paßt?

Beispiel
*Uli – **E***

Uli

Viel Obst und Gemüse essen, aber nicht zuviel Fett.

Thomas

Nicht zuviel essen – man sollte öfter weniger essen und viel Wasser trinken.

Katrin

Man sollte jede Menge Salat essen, und nicht zuviel Fleisch.

Andreas

Solange es dir schmeckt, ist alles gesund. Dieses Gerede vom gesunden Essen ist doch Quatsch. Ich esse alles!

Martina

Beate

Ich weiß, was gesundes Essen ist: frisches Obst, Salat, kein Fleisch usw., aber ich tu's einfach nicht. Wer tut das schon?!

Es ist schlecht, zwischen den Mahlzeiten zu essen, aber ich esse gerne zwischendurch Schokoriegel, Chips, Kekse und solche Sachen.

Und du?

Was meinst du?
Zeichne deine ideale gesunde Mahlzeit, und beschreib sie.

Steffi

Torsten

Es ist ungesund, zuviel Zucker zu essen, wie zum Beispiel Schokolade, Süßigkeiten, Kekse und Kuchen.

Kalorientabelle

Sieh dir die Kalorientabelle an.

Getränke	Kalorien
eine Tasse Tee ohne Milch	1
eine Tasse schwarzer Kaffee	3
eine Tasse Tee mit Milch	23
eine Tasse Kaffee mit Milch	25
(Zucker im Tee oder Kaffee)	+25
ein Glas Saft	33
ein Glas Cola	60
ein Glas Wein	68
ein Glas Bier	80
eine Tasse Kakao	170
ein Glas Milch	180
Cornflakes	
eine Schale	92
Brot	
eine Scheibe	60
Butter und Margarine	
eine Portion	37
Käse	
ein Stück	75
Eier	
ein gekochtes Ei	80
ein Spiegelei	136
Fisch	
ein Stück gegrillter Fisch	75
ein Stück gebratener Fisch	400

Fleisch	Kalorien
eine Bratwurst	160
ein Steak	168
ein Hamburger	260
Gemüse	
eine Portion Salat	5
eine Portion Karotten	20
eine Portion Erbsen	40
eine Portion Salzkartoffeln	140
eine Portion Pommes frites	260
Obst und Nüsse	
ein Apfel	35
eine Banane	45
250 g Nüsse	140
Suppen	
eine Portion Tomatensuppe	140
Kekse	
ein Keks	80
Kuchen	
ein Stück	300
Konfitüre	
ein Löffel Marmelade	25
ein Löffel Honig	30
ein Löffel Nutella	40
Bonbons und Chips	
ein Päckchen Kartoffelchips	140
ein Päckchen Gummibärchen	150
eine Tafel Schokolade	200

1 Wieviel Kalorien sind das?

2 Wieviel Kalorien nimmst du zu dir?
Was ißt du an einem typischen Tag?
Schreib eine Liste. Wieviel Kalorien sind das?

3 Schmeckt gut und ist gesund!
Schreib ein Menü mit weniger als 1 200 Kalorien pro Tag.

Tip des Tages

Wie oft ißt du Bonbons?
Wie oft trinkst du Limonade?

Sehr oft – dreimal bis viermal am Tag.
Oft – einmal bis zweimal am Tag.
Manchmal – einmal bis dreimal in der Woche.
Selten – einmal bis dreimal im Monat.
Nie – gar nicht.

Die Zahlen über 100	
101	hunderteins
102	hundertzwei
175	hundertfünfundsiebzig
250	zweihundertfünfzig
1 000	tausend
1 001	tausendeins
12 345	zwölftausenddreihundertfünfundvierzig
1 000 000	eine Million
2 000 000	zwei Millionen

sb ▸ *Selbstbedienung*

Lernziel 1

 Frühstückskarte

Welches Gedeck paßt zu welchem Foto?

Hotel Waldruh

FRÜHSTÜCKSKARTE

„Guten Morgen"

Gedeck I   DM
1 Tasse Kaffee, Tee oder Schokolade
1 Brötchen, Butter und Konfitüre
                                                6,90

Gedeck II
1 Tasse Kaffee, Tee oder Schokolade
2 Brötchen, Butter und Konfitüre
1 gekochtes Ei
                                                8,25

Gedeck III
1 Kännchen Kaffee, Tee oder Schokolade
2 Brötchen, Butter und gek. Schinken
                                                12,00

Lernziel 1

 Müsli, oder …?

*Was kann man hier
essen und trinken?
Wie ist es richtig?*
Beispiel
A – *Müsli*

Lernziel 2

 Namengedicht

*Lies das Gedicht, und füll die Lücken mit
reimenden Wörtern aus.*
Beispiel
Eine Apfelsine für Sabine.

Eine … für Sabine.
Käse mit … für Renate.
Toast mit … für Arabella.
Brötchen und … für Christine.
Eine Portion … für Ludwig.
Hähnchen mit Pommes … für Dorit.
Peperoni und … für Monika.

Kannst du weitere Beispiele schreiben?

Lernziel 2

 Briefe aus Spanien, Frankreich und Italien

Lies folgende Briefe, und schreib ‚richtig' oder ‚falsch'.

Benidorm, den 2. Juli

Liebe Katy!

Hallo! Wie geht's? Habt Ihr gutes Wetter? Hier ist das Wetter sehr schön.

Das Essen im Hotel ist nicht so gut. Das Brot zum Frühstück ist nicht frisch. Zu Mittag gibt's immer Fisch mit Reis. Das Abendessen schmeckt gut, aber die Portionen sind zu klein.

Bis nächste Woche!

Viele Grüße und Küsse,

Deine Gabi

Paris, den 10. Juni

Liebe Paula!

Jetzt bin ich schon drei Wochen hier. Ich finde es ganz toll hier in Paris. Das Frühstück im Hotel ist recht gut.

Mittags machen wir ein Picknick. Ich kaufe Obst, Käse und Brot und esse im Park. Das schmeckt toll! Abends esse ich in einem kleinen Café. Schade, daß Du nicht hier bist!

Herzliche Grüße

Deine

Dorit

Rom, den 4. August

Lieber Jürgen,

Rom ist eine tolle Stadt. Es gibt so viel zu sehen hier. Das Essen hier schmeckt fantastisch! (Nicht nur Ravioli) Es gibt frische, warme Brötchen zum Frühstück. Die Bäckerei ist neben dem Hotel. Mittags gibt es immer eine Suppe und viel, viel Fleisch! Abends gibt es ein kaltes Büffet mit Schinken, Wurst und Käse. Die Salate schmecken auch toll! Morgen gehe ich zum Kolosseum. Bis bald!

Dein Peter

---

1 Gabi findet das Frühstück toll.

2 Zum Abendessen sind die Portionen nicht groß genug.

3 Dorit macht gern Picknicks im Park.

4 Abends ißt sie im Hotel.

5 Peter findet das Essen in Rom toll.

6 Abends ißt er kalt.

Lernziel 3

 Picknickzeit!

Sieh dir die Kalorientabelle auf Seite 61 an, und plane ein Picknick für vier Personen. Wieviel Kalorien sind das?

Lernziel 3

 Ein Poster für gesundes Essen

Mal dein eigenes Poster für gesundes Essen.
Beispiel

Hamburger – nein, danke!

Bildvokabeln   **Zu Tisch!**

der Teelöffel

die Kanne

die Untertasse

die Tasse

der Löffel

die Serviette

das Set

der Servierlöffel

das Messer
die Gabel

der Pfeffer

das Salz

die Flasche

der Teller

die Schüssel

der Käseteller

der Tisch

die Tischdecke

auf einen Blick

1 Asking questions

Ißt du Toast?				Do you eat toast?		
Trinkst du Milch?				Do you drink milk?		
Was			Frühstück?	What		breakfast?
ißt du	zum		Mittagessen?	do you	for	lunch?
(gern)			Abendessen?	(like to) eat		dinner?
Wie oft ißt du		Bonbons?		How often do you eat sweets?		
		Süßigkeiten?				
Wie oft trinkst du Limonade?				How often do you drink lemonade?		

2 Saying what you like to eat and drink

Ich esse		Schokoriegel.	I like eating	chocolate bars.
	gern	Chips.		crisps.
		Kekse.		biscuits.
Ich trinke		Milch.	I like drinking	milk.
		Cola.		coke.

3 Numbers over 100

101	hunderteins	1 000	tausend	1 000 000	eine Million
102	hundertzwei	1 001	tausendeins	2 000 000	zwei Millionen
175	hundertfünfundsiebzig				
250	zweihundertfünfzig	12 345	zwölftausenddreihundertfünfundvierzig		

4 Talking about how often you do something

Sehr oft – dreimal bis viermal am Tag.	Very often – three to four times a day.
Oft – einmal bis zweimal am Tag.	Often – once to twice a day.
Manchmal – einmal bis dreimal in der Woche.	Sometimes – once to three times a week.
Selten – einmal bis dreimal im Monat.	Seldom – once to three times a month.
Nie – gar nicht.	Never – not at all.

5 Talking about healthy eating and expressing opinions

Man sollte	viel Obst und Gemüse	essen.	You should eat	lots of fruit and vegetables.
	öfter weniger			less but more often.
	jede Menge Salat			lots of salad.
	nicht zuviel Fett		You should not eat	too much fat.
	nicht zuviel			too much.
	viel Wasser	trinken.	You should drink	lots of water.

Solange es dir schmeckt, ist alles gesund.	As long as it's to your liking everything is healthy.
Dieses Gerede vom gesunden Essen ist doch Quatsch!	All this talk about healthy eating is rubbish!
Es ist ungesund, zuviel Zucker zu essen.	It's unhealthy to eat too much sugar.
Es ist schlecht, zwischen den Mahlzeiten zu essen.	It's bad to eat between meals.
Ich esse gerne etwas zwischendurch.	I like to eat something between meals.
Ich weiß, was gesundes Essen ist, aber ich tu's einfach nicht.	I know what healthy eating is, but I just don't do it.

Lernziel 1
Schulfächer und Schulaufgaben

 Welches Fach ist das?

Sieh dir die Schulfächer an.
Hör gut zu. Welches Fach ist das?
Beispiel
1 J *(Sport)*

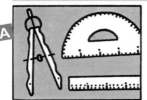
A — **Mathematik**

B — **Deutsch**

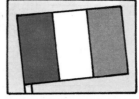
C — **Englisch**

D — **Französisch**

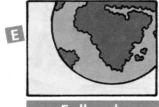
E — **Erdkunde**

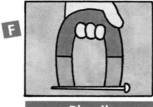
F — **Physik**

G — **Chemie**

H — **Biologie**

I — **Musik**

J — **Sport**

K — **Kunst**

L — **Sozialkunde**

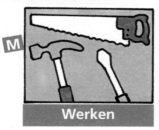
M — **Werken**

N — **Maschinenschreiben**

O — **Hauswirtschaft**

P — **Geschichte**

Purzelwörter

Schreib die Fächer auf.
Beispiel
A *Physik*

A HIPSKY
B CHINLEGS
C SICCTHEGHE
E DREDNEKU
F HIKTETAMAM
G SHUDTEC
H ILIEGOB

Schulaufgaben

Hier sind die Resultate einer Umfrage über Schüler und Schulaufgaben in Deutschland.

1 Wann machst du deine Schulaufgaben?

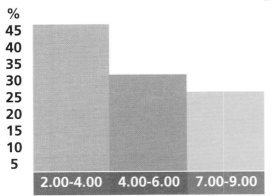

%			
45			
40			
35			
30			
25			
20			
15			
10			
5			
	2.00-4.00	4.00-6.00	7.00-9.00

Fünfundvierzig Prozent machen die Schulaufgaben nach dem Mittagessen zwischen zwei und vier Uhr.

Dreißig Prozent arbeiten nachmittags zwischen vier und sechs Uhr.

Fünfundzwanzig Prozent machen die Schulaufgaben nach dem Abendessen zwischen sieben und neun Uhr.

Partnerarbeit

A – Wieviel Prozent arbeiten nachmittags zwischen vier und sechs Uhr?
B – Dreißig Prozent. Wieviel arbeiten zwischen dreißig Minuten und anderthalb Stunden?
A – Dreißig Prozent.

Und du?

Wann machst du deine Schulaufgaben? Wie lange arbeitest du für die Schule?

2 Wie lange arbeitest du?

%			
45			
40			
35			
30			
25			
20			
15			
10			
5			
	30 Min. - 1½ Std.	1½ Std. - 2 Std.	2 Std. - 3 Std.

Dreißig Prozent arbeiten zwischen dreißig Minuten und anderthalb Stunden.

Fünfundvierzig Prozent arbeiten zwischen anderthalb und zwei Stunden.

Fünfundzwanzig Prozent arbeiten zwischen zwei und drei Stunden.

Eine gute Ausrede

Hör gut zu, und sieh dir die Bilder an.

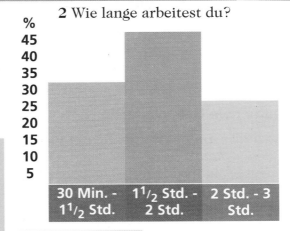

Tip des Tages

Was lernst du in der Schule?	
Ich lerne	Deutsch. Englisch. Französisch. Physik. Mathe (Mathemathik). Erdkunde. Geschichte. Kunst. Werken.
Wann machst du deine	Schulaufgaben? Hausaufgaben?
Zwischen fünf und halb sieben.	
Wie lange arbeitest du?	
Anderthalb Stunden.	

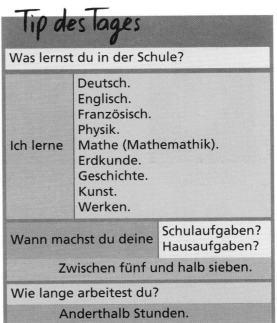

Lernziel 2
Lieblingsfächer

Partnerarbeit.
Was ist dein Lieblingsfach?

> Was ist dein Lieblingsfach?

> Mathe. Welches Fach gefällt dir gar nicht?

> Erdkunde.

> Englisch. Und dein Lieblingsfach?

> Französisch. Und dir?

Jetzt bist du dran.

Hast du heute dein Lieblingsfach?

Sieh dir die Bilder an, lies die Texte und füll die Tabelle aus.
Schreib ‚ja' oder ‚nein'.
1 Wer hat heute sein/ihr Lieblingsfach?
2 Welches Fach gefällt Helene/Jörg/Britta/Dirk gar nicht?
  Hat sie/er heute dieses Fach?

	Fach	
	1 ☺	2 ☹
Helene	*ja*	*nein*
Jörg		
Britta		
Dirk		

Beispiel

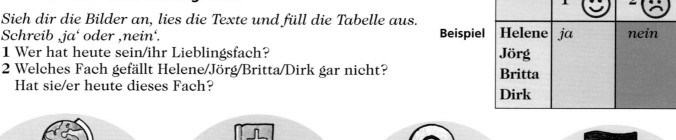

Helene

Jörg

Britta

Dirk

> Mein Lieblingsfach ist Erdkunde. Französisch gefällt mir gar nicht.

> Mein Lieblingsfach ist Musik. Chemie gefällt mir gar nicht.

> Mein Lieblingsfach ist Mathe. Geschichte gefällt mir gar nicht.

> Mein Lieblingsfach ist Deutsch. Religion gefällt mir gar nicht.

Sag mal

Hör gut zu. Wer spricht?
Wie ist die richtige Reihenfolge?
Beispiel – C, ...

C **Erdkunde? Super!**

D **Kunst gefällt mir gut.**

E **Religion gefällt mir gar nicht.**

B **Geschichte ist ganz interessant.**

F **Mathe? Ach, das geht.**

A **Französisch ist stinklangweilig!**

G **Musik finde ich toll!**

Sind die Bemerkungen ... ...?

	positiv	neutral	negativ
Beispiel	*super!*	*Das geht.*	*stinklangweilig*

Umfrage

Stell Fragen. Wie findest du ...?
Schreib die Antworten auf.

Eine schlechte Note

Hör gut zu und schreib Karins Noten auf.

Steffi

1 *Steffi! Steh auf!*

2 *Steffi! Es ist halb acht. Steh doch auf!*

Erdkunde—das ist das 'wo'. . .

3 *Aber das 'warum'— das machen wir nie!*

Geschichte—das ist das 'wann' und Wissenschaft das 'wie'. . .

Tip des Tages

Was ist dein Lieblingsfach?	
	Biologie.
Was sind deine Lieblingsfächer?	
	Mathe und Geschichte.
Welches Fach gefällt dir gar nicht?	
	Englisch.
Wie findest du Deutsch?	
	Super!
	Toll!
	(Ganz) interessant.
	Es gefällt mir gut.
	Das geht.
	(Stink)langweilig.

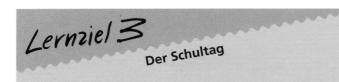

Lernziel 3

Der Schultag

Kirstens Stundenplan

Sieh dir den Stundenplan an.

Zeit	Montag	Dienstag	Mittwoch	Donnerstag	Freitag	Samstag
1 8.00 -8.45	Biologie	Französisch	Deutsch	Haus-wirtschaft	Geschichte	Physik
2 8.50 -9.35	Mathe	Englisch	Erdkunde	Haus-wirtschaft	Deutsch	Deutsch
9.35 -9.45	P	A	U	S	E	
3 9.45 -10.30	Deutsch	Mathe	Englisch	Mathe	Erdkunde	Maschinen-schreiben
4 10.35 -11.20	Geschichte	Sport	Französisch	Mathe	Englisch	Französisch
11.20 -11.35	P	A	U	S	E	
5 11.35 -12.20	Englisch	Kunst	Sozialkunde	Biologie	Werken	frei
6 12.25 -13.10	Physik	Kunst	Musik	frei	Werken	frei

Richtig oder falsch?

Beispiel

1 = *richtig*

1 Kirsten hat Biologie am Montag in der ersten Stunde.
2 Kirsten hat Kunst am Dienstag in den letzten zwei Stunden.
3 Sie hat Mathe am Montag in der letzten Stunde.
4 Sie hat Hauswirtschaft am Donnerstag in der dritten Stunde.
5 Sie hat zwei Stunden Werken am Freitag.
6 Sie hat erst vier Stunden am Samstag.
7 Sie hat Erdkunde zweimal am Mittwoch – in der zweiten und in der fünften Stunde.
8 Sie hat vier Stunden Mathe in der Woche.

Partnerarbeit. Welcher Tag?

Wähl einen Tag vom Stundenplan, und beantworte die Fragen mit ‚ja' oder ‚nein'.
A – Ja, fertig.
B – Hast du Geschichte?
A – Ja.
B – Und hast du Physik?
A – Nein.
B – Ist es Freitag?
A – Ja. Jetzt bist du dran.

Die erste Stunde fällt aus!

He du! Die erste Stunde fällt aus!

Oh danke. Tschüs!

Die erste Stunde fällt aus!

Oh toll! Danke. Tschüs!

Großbritannien oder Deutschland?

Wo sind die Teenager? In Deutschland oder in Großbritannien?

Jetzt bist du dran.
Du telefonierst mit deinen Klassenkameraden.
Hier sind die Telefonnummern:

1	a	207625	6	a	71684	11	a	6318
	b	6318		b	2742		b	14404
2	a	2742	7	a	78103	12	a	17744
	b	2332		b	26924		b	32367
3	a	24747	8	a	62948	13	a	25240
	b	78103		b	24747		b	72201
4	a	14404	9	a	91026	14	a	32367
	b	91026		b	71684		b	25240
5	a	26924	10	a	2332	15	a	72201
	b	17744		b	62948		b	207625

1

Wir haben keine Schuluniform.

2

Wir haben samstags keine Schule.

Die Schule ist meistens um ein Uhr aus.

Wir essen nicht zu Mittag in der Schule.

Nachmittags haben wir drei Stunden.

6

3

4

5

6	1.35 – 2.10
7	2.15 – 2.50
8	2.55 – 3.30

Unsere Klassenlehrer unterrichten alle zwei Fächer.

Die erste Stunde ist um Viertel vor neun zu Ende.

8

9

Wir bleiben meistens in unserem Klassenraum, und der Lehrer kommt zu uns.

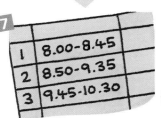

7

1	8.00 – 8.45
2	8.50 – 9.35
3	9.45 – 10.30

Meine Schwester ist fünf Jahre alt und geht noch nicht zur Schule.

Wir haben jeden Tag eine Versammlung in der Aula.

10

Tip des Tages

Was hast du Was hat Kirsten	in der	ersten zweiten dritten letzten	Stunde?	Ich habe Sie hat	Biologie. Religion. Musik. Sport.

sb ▶ Selbstbedienung

Lernziel 1

 **Was haben sie auf?**

Schreib die Fächer auf.
Beispiel
1 *Englisch*

Lernziel 1

Kochen? Köstlich!

Welche Wörter gehören zusammen.
Schlag in der Wörterliste nach.
Beispiel
Kochen? Köstlich!

Kochen
Sport
Kunst
Musik
Französisch
Latein

Englisch
Chemie
Werken
Erdkunde
Deutsch
Informatik

einfach
interessant
langweilig
dumm
fein
köstlich
fantastisch
kreativ
mies

super
stinklangweilig
doof
lustig
melodisch
katastrophal
wunderbar
chaotisch
ernstlich

Lernziel 2

Lieblingsfächer, oder …?

Was sagen die Teenager?
Beispiel
Jutta: Biologie ist mein Lieblingsfach.
Englisch gefällt mir gar nicht.

Schlüssel

= Lieblingsfach

= gefällt mir gar nicht

Anne

Bernd

Anke

Sven

Jutta

Deutsch Mathe Biologie Geschichte Englisch

Selbstbedienung sb

Lernziel 3

Lernziel 3

 **Fragen und Antworten**

Was gehört zusammen?
Beispiel 1C

1	Wann hast du heute Biologie?		**A**	Es geht.
2	Was sind deine Lieblingsfächer?		**B**	Acht.
3	Wie gefällt dir Mathematik?		**C**	In der sechsten Stunde.
4	Was hast du in der dritten Stunde?		**D**	Herr Backmann.
5	Wie heißt dein Deutschlehrer?		**E**	Biologie und Kunst.
6	Wieviel Stunden hast du am Tag?		**F**	Um elf Uhr.
7	Wann ist die Pause?		**G**	Englisch.

Lernziel 3

 Hauptschule, Realschule ...?

Sieh dir die Stundenpläne an.
Auf welche Schule gehen diese Schüler? Auf die
Hauptschule, die Realschule, die Gesamtschule
oder das Gymnasium?
Beispiel 1 – *Das Gymnasium*

1 Ich habe am Samstag nur vier Stunden. Um elf Uhr zehn ist die Schule aus.

2 Mein Lieblingsfach ist Biologie. Leider haben wir nur drei Stunden in der Woche.

3 Politik ist toll, aber Kunst finde ich ein bißchen langweilig.

4 Samstage sind für mich schulfrei. Gut, nicht?

5 Französisch und Kunst sind meine Lieblingsfächer. Donnerstag ist also mein Lieblingstag.

6 Ich singe sehr gern, also bleibe ich mittwochs ein bißchen länger in der Schule.

7 Geschichte gefällt mir gar nicht. Montags und mittwochs finde ich also nicht so gut.

8 Mathe ist schwierig. Mittwochs nach zwei Stunden bin ich kaputt!

Die Gesamtschule

Zeit	Montag	Dienstag	Mittwoch	Donnerstag	Freitag	Samstag
8.20-9.05	Naturw.	Deutsch	Religion	Wiss.	Tutor.	
9.10-9.55	Religion	Deutsch	Naturw.	Wiss.	Politik	
10.15-11.00	Werken	Franz.	Englisch	Franz.	Mathe	
11.05-11.50	Werken	Franz.	Englisch	Englisch	Mathe	
12.00-12.45	frei	Politik	frei	Deutsch	Englisch	
12.55-13.40	Franz.	Mathe	Deutsch	frei	frei	
13.50-14.35	Kunst	—	Mathe	Politik	Wiss.	
14.40-15.25	Musik	—	Sport	Rudern	—	
15.35-16.20	Wiss.	—	Sport	Rudern	—	

Die Realschule

Zeit	Mo	Di	Mi	Do	Fr	Sa
8.00-8.45	Deutsch	Chemie	Mathe	Englisch	frei	Englisch
8.50-9.35	Deutsch	Franz.	Mathe	Englisch	Mathe	Englisch
9.55-10.40	Physik	Biologie	Deutsch	Kunst	Gesch.	Mathe
10.45-11.30	Franz.	Englisch	Sport	Kunst	Deutsch	Mathe
11.45-12.30	Reli.	Erdkd.	Hauswirtsch.	Franz.	Sport	frei
12.20-13.10	Gesch	Erdkd.	Hauswirtsch.	Franz.	Sport	frei
	—	—	Hauswirtsch.	—	—	—
	—	—	Hauswirtsch.	—	—	—

Das Gymnasium

	Zeit	Montag	Dienstag	Mittwoch	Donn.	Freitag	Samstag
1	7.45-8.30	Englisch	frei	Sport	Franz.	Musik	Erdkunde
2	8.35-9.20	Deutsch	Englisch	Biologie	Deutsch	Franz.	Erdkunde
3	9.25-10.10	Musik	Religion	Englisch	Englisch	Mathe	Zeichnen
4	10.25-11.10	Franz.	Franz.	Franz.	Religion	Sport	Zeichnen
5	11.15-12.00	Mathe	Biologie	Deutsch	Mathe	Deutsch	frei
6	12.05-12.50	frei	frei	Chor (AG)	frei	frei	frei
N1	14.10-14.55		Mathe		Geschichte		
N2	15.00-15.45		Erdkunde		Sport		
N3	16.00-16.45		Geschichte				

Die Hauptschule

	Mo	Di	Mi	Do	Fr	Sa
1	Eng.	Dt.	Eng.	Bio	frei	Mathe
2	Mathe	Dt.	Eng.	Eng.	Dt.	Mathe
3	Mathe	Phys.	Mathe	Phys.	Dt.	Bio.
4	Gesch.	Erdk.	Gesch.	Erdk.	Kurzschrift	Mus.
5	Bio.	Kunst	Gesch.	Hausw.	Kurzschrift	Reli.
6	Mus.	Kunst	Reli.	Hausw.	Sport	frei
7			Nähen		Sport	
8			Nähen			

Bildvokabeln

In der Sportstunde

Handball

der Speerwurf

der Weitsprung

das Trampolin

Federball

der Hochsprung

der Hundertmeterlauf

Im Informatikraum

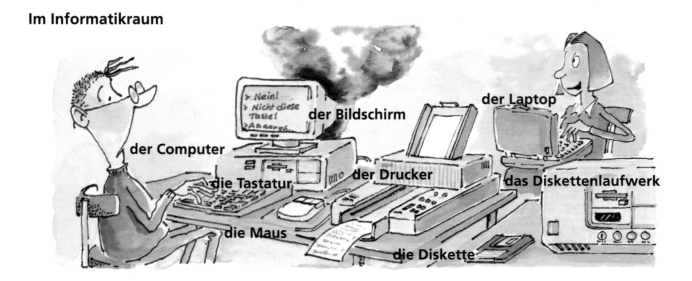

der Bildschirm

der Laptop

der Computer

der Drucker

das Diskettenlaufwerk

die Tastatur

die Maus

die Diskette

1 Asking questions

Was lernst du in der Schule?			What subjects do you take at school?		
Was hast du heute auf?			What homework have you got today?		
Wann machst du deine	Schulaufgaben? Hausaufgaben?		When do you do your homework?		
Wie lange arbeitest du?			How long do you work?		
Was ist dein Lieblingsfach?			What is your favourite subject?		
Was sind deine Lieblingsfächer?			What are your favourite subjects?		
Wie findest du Deutsch?			What do you think of German?		
Welches Fach gefällt dir gar nicht?			Which subject don't you like at all?		
Was hast du in der	ersten zweiten	Stunde?	What have you got	first second	lesson?

auf einen Blick

2 Talking about school subjects

Ich lerne	Deutsch. Physik. Mathe. Erdkunde. Musik. Kunst. Religion.	I take	German. physics. maths. geography. music. art. R.E.
Mein Lieblingsfach ist Mathe.		My favourite subject is maths.	
Meine Lieblingsfächer sind Deutsch und Chemie.		My favourite subjects are German and chemistry.	
Englisch gefällt mir gut.		I like English.	
Chemie ist	toll! super! ganz interessant. (stink)langweilig.	Chemistry is	great! super! quite interesting. (dead) boring.
Kunst? Das geht.		Art? It's all right.	
Musik gefällt mir gar nicht.		I don't like music at all.	

3 Talking about your school day/timetable

Ich habe	Musik Chemie Deutsch Biologie	in der	zweiten dritten vierten letzten	Stunde.	I've got	music chemistry German biology	in the	2nd 3rd 4th last	lesson.

Lernziel 1
Sport und Hobbys

🔲 **Interviews nach der Schule**

Hör gut zu. Welches Bild paßt?
Beispiel
1D

Ich spiele mit dem Computer

Ich spiele Basketball.

Ich höre Musik.

Ich spiele Tennis.

Ich sehe fern.

Ich spiele Klavier.

Ich gehe mit dem Hund spazieren.

Ich treffe mich mit meinen Freunden.

Ich lese.

Ich bummle in der Stadt.

Ich sortiere meine Briefmarken.

Ich fahre mit dem Rad.

Ich reite.

Ich spiele Fußball.

Ich gehe schwimmen.

Ich gehe in die Disco.

🔴🔴 **Partnerarbeit**

Wähl ein Bild und stell eine Frage.
Dein(e) Partner(in) muß die Frage beantworten.
Beispiel
A – Was machst du in deiner Freizeit? Bild A?
B – Ich spiele mit dem Computer. Was machst du in deiner Freizeit? Bild H?
A – …

🎧 Computerpartner

Hier sind zehn Jungen und Mädchen.
Hör gut zu. Der Computer gibt dir Informationen über sie
und ihre Hobbys.
Wer hat deine Hobbys? Wer ist dein(e) Computerpartner(in)?

Murat

Anne

Raphaela

Torsten

Uschi

Florian

Bernd

Peter

Asla

Brigitte

Beste Freunde 🎧

Hör zu und lies das Gedicht.

Hab' einen Freund,
der wohnt in Hof.
Furchtbar nett,
furchtbar doof.

Hab' eine Freundin,
die wohnt in Bern.
Hat keine Hobbys,
guckt nur fern.

Hab' einen Freund,
der wohnt in Kiel.
Trinkt wie ein Fisch
und isst zuviel.

Hab' eine Freundin,
die wohnt in Trier.
Geht gern tanzen
– nicht mit mir!

Hab' einen Freund,
der wohnt in Essen.
Was macht er gern?
Ich hab's vergessen.

Freunde und
Freundinnen überall.
Wie sie sind,
ist mir egal!

Tip des Tages

Was machst du in deiner Freizeit?

Ich	spiele	(gern)	Fußball. Tennis. Basketball. Klavier. mit dem Computer.
	höre sehe gehe		Musik. fern. in die Disco.

Lernziel 2
Fernsehen

1
Das ist eine Musiksendung.

2
Das ist eine Sportsendung.

3
Das ist ein Film.

4
Das ist die Werbung.

5
Das ist eineNatursendung.

6
Das sind die Nachrichten.

🔊 Ich sehe gern fern

Sieh dir die Fernsehsendungen an, und hör gut zu.
Welche Sendungen sind das?
Beispiel
1: 3, 7

◖◗ Und du?

Wie findest du diese Sendungen?
Mach einen Dialog mit deinem Partner/deiner Partnerin.
Beispiel
A – Wie findest du Sportsendungen?
B – Doof. Und du?
A – Toll!
B – Wie findest du Trickfilme?
A – Komisch. Und du?
B – Nicht schlecht.

◖◗ Partnerarbeit. Fernsehsendungen

Sieh dir die Bilder und Texte an.
Beispiel
A – Welche Fernsehsendung ist das? Nummer eins?
B – Das ist eine Musiksendung.

7
Das ist eine Serie.

8
Das ist ein Schauspiel.

9
Das ist eine Komödie.

10
Das ist ein Trickfilm.

11
Das ist eine Spielshow.

12
Das ist eine Talkshow.

Tip des Tages

Wie findest du	Serien?
	Werbung?
	Musiksendungen?
	Trickfilme?
Siehst du gern	Talkshows?
	Nachrichten?
	Komödien?
	prima.
	toll.
	gut.
	interessant.
(Sie sind)	nicht schlecht.
	komisch.
	doof.
	blöd.
	stinklangweilig.

Hören und Sehen

Sieh dir die Programmzeitschrift an.
Was für Sendungen gibt es?
Schreib die Kategorien auf,
und mach Listen.

Beispiel Kindersendungen – *baff*
Musiksendungen
Sportsendungen
Filme
Natursendungen
Schauspiele
Talkshows
Spielshows
Nachrichten
Dokumentarfilme
Komödien

SAT 1

15.00	**Tagesschau**
15.03	**baff**
	Ein Kindermagazin
	Kindersendung ab 6 Jahren
15.30	**Dick und Doof**
15.35	**Trick 7**
	Die besten Zeichentrickfilme
	ab 7 Jahren
	Familie Feuerstein
	Tiny Toon Abenteuer
16.00	**FILM: Kidnapping in New York**
	Amerikanischer Krimi
17.15	**Tagesschau**
17.30	**Geh aufs Ganze**
	Spielshow
18.00	**Sport heute**
	Sportnachrichten und -berichte
19.15	**Tante Trude aus Buxtehude**
	Deutsche Komödie

ZDF

15.00	**Alles klar**
	Reisetips
	Heute: Madrid
15.30	**Hopp oder Topp**
	Spielshow
16.00	**Sporthelden**
	Die besten Fußballer der Welt
16.55	**5 vor 5**
	Kurznachrichten mit Sport und Wetter
17.00	**Tennis**
	Turnier in Kiel
	Ein Leckerbissen für alle Tennisfans
18.00	FILM: **Durch dick und dünn**
	Französischer Krimi

RTL

15.00	**Dschungelbuch**
	Zeichentrickfilm
16.30	**Ruck Zuck**
	Spielshow
17.00	**Step-Aerobic**
	Fitness-Programm zum Mitmachen
17.30	**Nie mehr nach Hause**
	Reportage über Straßenkinder in Deutschland
18.30	**Studiodiskussion zum Thema Straßenkinder**

Streit

Rifat und Cigden streiten immer über Fernsehsendungen.
Hör zu. Was will Rifat sehen? Und Cigden?
Schreib zwei Listen.
Beispiel

Rifat	Cigden
baff	*Dschungelbuch*

 **Superglotzer der Woche**

Mach eine Klassenumfrage.
Wer ist Superglotzer in deiner Klasse?
Beispiel
A – Wie lange siehst du montags fern?
B – Ungefähr eine Stunde.
A – Und dienstags/mittwochs/donnerstags/ freitags/samstags/sonntags?
B – Zwei Stunden/...
A – Das macht wieviel Stunden insgesamt pro Woche?
B – Zwanzig Stunden.

Lernziel 3

Was machst du am liebsten?

*Sieh dir die Statistik an.
Was machen die Jugendlichen
am liebsten in der Freizeit?
Wieviel Prozent hören am
liebsten Musik?
Und wieviel spielen am
liebsten Fußball?*

Musik hören 24%

Fernsehen 21%

Freunde treffen 18%

Schwimmen 15%

Fußball spielen 10%

Computer spielen 5%

Lesen 4%

Basketball 3%

*Und du? Was machst du
am liebsten in der Freizeit?*

BRITTA TELL – ein Profil

Lies das Profil

Evi Bamm

Britta XXX

Lieblingssänger(in): Evi Bamm
Lieblingslied: BLITZ
Lieblingsfarbe: ROT!
Lieblingsfach in der Schule: Musik
Lieblingssport: Tennis
Lieblingssportler(in): Boris Becker
Lieblingsgericht: Spaghetti
Lieblingsgetränk: Rotwein
Lieblingsfilm: Der mit dem Wolf tanzt
Lieblingsmotto: Tu immer dein Bestes

Tip des Tages

Was machst du am liebsten in der Freizeit?		
Am liebsten	höre ich spiele ich	Musik. Tennis.
	lese ich.	
Wer ist dein(e) Lieblingssportler(in)?		
Mein Lieblingssportler ist Boris Becker. Meine Lieblingssportlerin ist Steffi Graf.		

Schreib jetzt dein eigenes Profil.

Was für Musik hörst du am liebsten?

Sieh dir die Fotos und Texte an.
Was meinst du – wer sagt was?
Hör zu – die Antworten sind auf
Kassette.

Hatice

Sonja

Stefan

Florian

Murat

Ich spiele in einem Orchester.
Am liebsten spiele ich
klassische Musik.

Ich spiele kein Instrument, aber ich
höre gern Musik. Am liebsten höre
ich Jazz oder Chansons.

Am liebsten höre
ich Popmusik.

Ich gehe oft in die Disco.
Am liebsten höre
ich Tanzmusik.

Ich bin in einer Rockgruppe.
Die Gruppe heißt Metal Hammer.
Meine Lieblingsmusik ist
natürlich Rock!

In meiner Freizeit

Hör zu und sing mit.

Was machst du nach der Schule?
Naja, es tut mir leid,
Ich möchte gerne kommen,
Doch ich hab' keine Zeit.

Eine Stunde Hausaufgaben,
Manchmal zwei.
In meiner Freizeit
Bin ich niemals frei!

Ich spiele gern Gitarre,
Hab' jedoch wenig Zeit.
Ich gehe gern spazieren,
Doch ich komme nie sehr weit.

Eine Stunde Hausaufgaben,
Manchmal zwei.
In meiner Freizeit
Bin ich niemals frei!

Ich gehe nicht mehr schwimmen,
Und ich schwimme doch so gern.
Ich gehe nie ins Kino.
Ich sehe selten fern.

Zwei Stunden
Hausaufgaben,
Manchmal drei.
In meiner Freizeit
Bin ich niemals ...
Bist du niemals ...
Bin ich niemals frei!

sb ▷ *Selbstbedienung*

Lernziel 1

 Was machst du?

Was sagen die Leute?
Schreib die Antworten auf.
Beispiel
1 *Ich fahre mit dem Rad.*

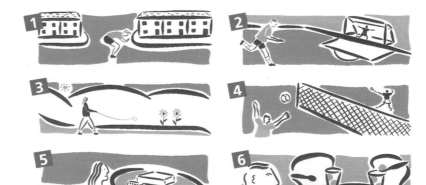

Lernziel 1

Treffpunkt

Was für Brieffreunde willst du haben? Schreib deine Hobbys auf, dann lies die Anzeigen. Wer paßt am besten zu dir?

TREFFPUNKT

Ich bin fünfzehn und suche nette Brieffreunde oder Brieffreundinnen zwischen vierzehn und sechzehn. Hobbys: Musik, Tischtennis, Tanzen, Kino. Schreibt mit Foto an Jochen Schmidt, Nelkenstraße 2, 93053

Bist du sportlich? Bist du vierzehn? Bist du ein Junge? Wenn ja, dann schreib mir doch und leg ein Foto von dir bei. Meine Interessen sind Tennis, Basketball, Squash, Schwimmen und Radfahren. Meine Adresse: Karin Rosenberg, Altwiesenstraße 80, CH-8051 Zürich.

Ich suche Brieffreunde zwischen zwölf und vierzehn. Hobbys: Kochen, Schwimmen, Lesen, Turnen. Bitte schreibt mit Foto an Britta Wolff, Immweg 22, 38120 Braunschweig.

Hallo. Ich bin fünfzehn. Meine Hobbys sind Schlagzeugspielen, Tanzen, Sport, Musik. (Meine Lieblingssängerin ist Evi Bamm.) Für alle interessierten Mädchen ist meine Adresse: Siegfried Voigt, Münsterstr. 13, 47798 Krefeld.

Welches Mädchen im Alter von zwölf bis vierzehn möchte mir schreiben? Meine Hobbys sind Fußball, Schach, Briefmarken, Spazierengehen und Computer. Schreibt bitte an Stephan Wirgler, Kameterstraße 51/3, A-1211 Wien. (Wenn möglich, schickt ein Foto mit.)

Wer möchte mir schreiben? Ich bin sechzehn Jahre alt und ein Skorpionmädchen. Meine Hobbys sind Rollschuhlaufen, Bummeln, Musik (Ede Funk ist mein Lieblingssänger), und Faulenzen. Bitte schreibt mit Foto an Sabine Fischer, Rostocker Straße 71/322, 70376 Stuttgart.

Einsamer Junge sucht süßes Mädchen. Ich bin fünfzehn und meine Hobbys sind Klavierspielen, klassische Musik und Jazz, Lesen und Kino. Schreibt mit Foto an Martin Gelten, Alfelderstraße 9, 28207 Bremen.

Ich bin dreizehn und suche Brieffreunde und Brieffreundinnen zwischen dreizehn und siebzehn. Hobbys: Rockmusik (Metal Hammer ist meine Lieblingsgruppe), Gitarre, Fernsehen, Schwimmen und Kino. Über Briefe mit Fotos würde ich mich freuen. Claudia Hildebrand, In den Kolkwiesen 61, 30851 Langenhagen 1.

Jetzt bist du dran. Schreib an TREFFPUNKT, und beschreib dich selbst – mit Foto!

Lernziel 2

 Was machst du gern nach der Schule?

Lies die Sätze, und sieh dir die Bilder an.
Was paßt zu wem?

Beispiel
1d

1 Nach der Schule ...
was ich gern mache?
Naja, ich gehe schwimmen.

2 Äh, ich spiele Tennis.
Wir haben eine Tennishalle
ganz in der Nähe.

3 Hmm, das ist schwer. Ich
habe kein festes Hobby. Ich
gehe aber abends in die
Disco.

4 Wenn ein guter Film im Kino
läuft, gehe ich gern ins Kino.

5 Nichts besonderes. Ich
bleibe gern zu Hause und
sehe gern fern.

Lernziel 2

 Stimmt das?

Sieh dir die Programmzeitschrift auf Seite 79 an.
Lies folgende Sätze, und schreib ‚richtig‘ oder ‚falsch‘.

1 *Alles klar* beginnt um drei Uhr nachmittags.
2 Heute gibt es keine Sendungen für Kinder.
3 Heute gibt es mindestens vier Spielshows zu sehen.
4 Im ZDF kann man mehr Sportsendungen sehen.
5 Heute sind zwei Krimis im Fernsehen zu sehen.
6 *Die Tagesschau* dauert immehr fünfzehn Minuten.
7 Es gibt keine Komödie heute abend.

Lernziel 3

 **Mein Freizeitwappen**

Mach dein eigenes Freizeitwappen.

Lernziel 3

 Aber am liebsten ...

Schreib die Sätze fertig.
Beispiel
1 *Karin liest gern und spielt gern Squash,*
aber am liebsten spielt sie Klavier.

1 Karin liest gern und spielt gern Squash,
aber am liebsten ...

2 Boris spielt gern Fußball und Basketball,
aber am liebsten ...

3 Lars bummelt gern in der Stadt und trifft
sich gern mit Freunden, aber am liebsten ...

4 Regina sieht gern fern und spielt gern mit
dem Computer, aber am liebsten ...

Bildvokabeln
Musikinstrumente

das Schlagzeug

das Keyboard

das Klavier

die Klarinette

die Trompete

die Blockflöte

die Flöte

die Gitarre

die Geige

das Saxophon

Steffi

Zum letzten Mal— das ist zu laut!

Es ist alles so still da oben—das ist nicht normal.

1 Asking questions

Was machst du in deiner Freizeit?	*What do you do in your spare time?*
Wie findest du Musiksendungen?	*What do you think of music programmes?*
Was willst du sehen?	*What do you want to watch?*
Wann ist der Film?	*When is the film on?*
Wie lange siehst du fern?	*(For) how long do you watch TV?*
Was machst du am liebsten in der Freizeit?	*What do you like doing best of all in your spare time?*
Was für Musik hörst du am liebsten?	*What kind of music do you most like to listen to?*

auf einen Blick

2 Talking about what you do in your spare time

Ich	spiele	Fußball. Tennis. Basketball. Klavier. mit dem Computer.	*I*	*play*	*football.* *tennis.* *basketball.* *the piano.* *on the computer.*
	höre	Musik.		*listen to*	*music.*
	sehe	fern.		*watch*	*TV.*
	gehe	in die Disco.		*go*	*to the disco.*

3 Expressing your opinion

Talkshows		interessant.	*Chatshows*		*interesting.*
Serien		toll.	*Soaps/serials*		*great.*
Natursendungen	sind	doof.	*Nature programmes*	*are*	*daft.*
Trickfilme		blöd.	*Cartoons*		*stupid.*
Nachrichten		stinklangweilig.	*News programmes*		*dead(ly) boring.*

4 Saying what you like doing, and what you like doing best of all

Ich	lese	gern.		*I like*	*reading.*	
	sehe	gern	fern.		*watching TV.*	
	spiele		Tennis.		*playing tennis.*	
Am liebsten	höre ich Musik. gehe ich schwimmen. gehe ich mit dem Hund spazieren.			*Most of all I like*	*listening to music.* *going swimming.* *taking the dog for a walk.*	

Was kostet das?

 Geld

*Hör zu. Einige Leute sprechen über Preise.
Wo sind die Leute? In Deutschland?
In Österreich? In der Schweiz?*
Beispiel
1 *Deutschland*

Lernziel 1

Geld und Preise

Münzen und Scheine

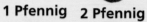
 1 Pfennig   **2 Pfennig**

 5 Pfennig   **10 Pfennig**

 50 Pfennig   **1 Mark**

 2 Mark **5 Mark**

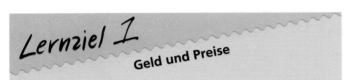

Das Geld in Deutschland

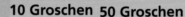   **10 Groschen 50 Groschen**

Das Geld in Österreich

  1 Schilling 5 Schilling

 10 Schilling

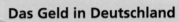

5 Rappen 10 Rappen

20 Rappen 50 Rappen

Das Geld in der Schweiz

 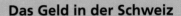

1 Franken 5 Franken

Partnerarbeit. Was kostet das?

Sieh dir die Artikel an. Stell Fragen.

Beispiel

A – Was kostet ein T-Shirt?
B – Zwanzig Mark. Was kosten die Bonbons?
A – …

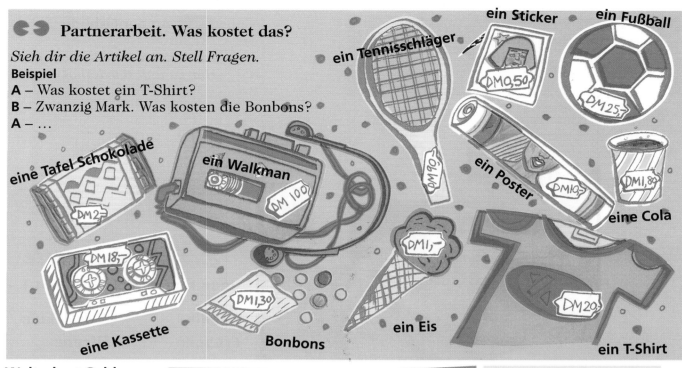

ein Tennisschläger · ein Sticker · ein Fußball
eine Tafel Schokolade · ein Walkman · ein Poster · eine Cola
eine Kassette · Bonbons · ein Eis · ein T-Shirt

Welt ohne Geld

Hör zu und sing mit.

1
Von Hand zu Hand, von Land zu Land
Geht es in einem Kreis.
Jedoch der Arme auf der Welt,
Der bezahlt den Preis.

Eine Welt ohne Geld,
Da könnte man leben.
Eine Welt ohne Geld,
Nun das wäre fein!
Eine Welt ohne Geld,
Das wird es nie geben.
Eine Welt ohne Geld,
So wird es nie sein.

2
Der eine gibt zehntausend aus,
Das ist nur ein Spiel.
Der andere braucht ein Stückchen Brot,
Ihm kostet das zuviel.

Eine Welt ohne Geld, ………

3
Der eine war ein reicher Mann,
Heute hat er nichts mehr.
Der andere fing als Bettler an
Und ist jetzt Millionär.

Eine Welt ohne Geld, ………

Tip des Tages

Was kostet	das?	2 Mark 50.
	ein Fußball?	40 Mark.
	eine Cola?	10 Schilling.
	ein T-Shirt?	20 Franken.
Was kosten	die Bonbons?	80 Pfennig.

Kann ich hier Geld wechseln?
Was wollen Sie denn wechseln?
Ich möchte 25 Pfund in D-Mark umwechseln.

Lernziel 2

Ich habe Hunger!

An der Eisbude

Diese Leute bestellen ein Eis.
Hör zu und wiederhol.

Hier, bitte, einmal Vanille und einmal Schokolade. Zwei Mark.

Einmal Vanille und einmal Schokolade, bitte.

Zweimal Erdbeer und zweimal Schokolade, bitte.

So. Zweimal Erdbeer und zweimal Schokolade. Vier Mark.

Eis – Preisliste

Jede Kugel nach Wahl DM 1,–

Vanille	**Schokolade**
Erdbeer	**Zitrone**
Mokka	**Himbeer**

Was nimmst du?

Was bestellen die Leute?
Hör zu.
Beispiel
1C

Partnerarbeit. An der Wurstbude

Mach Dialoge.

Beispiel

A – Was kostet eine Portion Pommes (frites)?

B – Zwei Mark fünfzig. Kann man hier Chips kaufen?

A – …

Die neue Kellnerin

Diese Kellnerin hat ihren ersten Arbeitstag.
Was macht sie richtig?
Was macht sie falsch?

Beispiel

A *richtig*

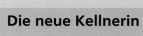

Tip des Tages

Was nimmst du?					
			(Ich nehme) (Ich hätte gern) (Ich möchte)	einen Hamburger, einen Apfelsaft, eine Bratwurst, eine Cola, eine Limonade, eine Tafel Schokolade, ein Schaschlik, ein Eis, ein belegtes Brot, zweimal Pommes (frites) mit Ketchup,	bitte.
Einmal Zweimal Dreimal	Vanille, Schokolade, Zitrone,	bitte.			

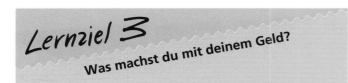

Lernziel 3

Was machst du mit deinem Geld?

🔊 Ich gebe mein Geld für CDs aus

Hier ist das Resultat von einer Umfrage über Jugendliche und Geld.

Hör gut zu.
Wofür geben die Teenager ihr Geld aus?
Schreib die Kategorien auf.
Beispiel
1 *Hobbys*

Umfrage

Mach jetzt eine Umfrage.
Schreib die Kategorien auf.
Beispiel
A – *Wofür gibst du dein Geld aus?*
B – *Ich gebe mein Geld für Kleider aus.*

🔊 Wofür sparst du dein Geld?

Sieh dir die Bilder an, und hör gut zu.
Wofür sparen die Leute?
Beispiel
1 E *(Computer)*

📼 Kommst du mit zum Jahrmarkt?

Gehst du gern zum Jahrmarkt?
Fährst du gern mit dem Riesenrad?
Sieh dir die Bilder an, und hör zu.
Was machen die Teenager gern, und was
machen sie am liebsten?

die Geisterbahn

das Riesenrad

die Schiffschaukel

das Karussell

die Achterbahn

der Autoscooter

	gern	am liebsten
Beispiel 1	*Riesenrad*	*Geisterbahn*

Tip des Tages

Wofür gibst du dein Geld aus?		
Ich gebe mein Geld für	Kleider Hobbys CDs Bonbons und Snacks	aus.

Fährst du gern mit	dem	Autoscooter? Riesenrad? Karussell?
	der	Achterbahn? Schiffschaukel?

Wofür sparst du dein Geld?	
Ich spare für	einen Computer. eine Gitarre. ein Fahrrad. neue Turnschuhe.
	Ja, aber am liebsten fahre ich mit der Geisterbahn.

sb  Selbstbedienung

Lernziel 1

 Wieviel ist das zusammen?

Sieh dir die Scheine und Münzen und die Geldsummen an. Wieviel macht das?

Beispiel
1 a

1
a fünfundzwanzig Mark
b fünfundzwanzig Schilling
c fünfundzwanzig Pfennig

2
a fünfzehn Schilling
b fünfzehn Mark
c fünfzig Schilling

3
a zehn Franken, fünfzig Rappen
b zwölf Mark vierzig
c zehn Mark fünfzig

4
a dreiundzwanzig Mark
b zweiunddreißig Franken
c dreiundzwanzig Franken

5
a achtzig Mark
b achtzig Franken
c achtzehn Schilling

6
a tausend Mark
b hundert Schilling
c hundert Franken

Lernziel 1

 Kostet? Kosten?

Vervollständige die Sätze mit ‚kostet‘ oder ‚kosten‘. Dann sieh dir die Bilder an, und schreib die Preise auf.

Beispiel
1 *Was kostet der Computer? Der Computer kostet tausend Mark.*

1 Was —— der Computer?
2 Was —— die Kassette?
3 Was —— die Turnschuhe?
4 Was —— das Eis?
5 Was —— die Bonbons?
6 Was —— der Film?

Lernziel 2

 Zweimal Cola, bitte

Was sagst du am Schnellimbiß?
Sieh dir die Bilder an, und schreib dieAntworten auf.

Beispiel
a *Zweimal Cola, bitte.*

Selbstbedienung sb

Lernziel 2

Am Schnellimbiß

Sieh dir die Bilder und den Text an.
Was kostet alles? Schreib die Preise auf.
Was bezahlen die Leute? Füll die
Sprechblasen aus.

Lernziel 3

Wofür gibst du dein Geld aus?

Wie ist das richtig?
Schreib die Sätze in der richtigen Reihenfolge auf.
Wer sagt was? Lies die Bemerkungen, und schreib
die passenden Namen auf.

Beispiel
1 Ich gebe mein Geld meistens für Bücher
und Kassetten aus. (Barbara)

Kassetten Bücher meistens gebe und gebe Geld mein für aus Ich	mein gebe Ich meine aus Geld Hobbys für	für Kleider Geld mein Make-up und Ich gebe aus	gebe Ich viel aus nicht	Ausgehen gebe ziemlich Ich viel beim Geld aus

Anton:

gibt sein Geld beim Ausgehen aus.

Kirsten:

gibt nicht viel aus.

Dieter:

gibt sein Geld für seine Hobbys aus.

Barbara:

gibt ihr Geld meistens für Bücher und Kassetten aus.

Marga:

gibt ihr Geld für Kleider und Make-up aus.

Bildvokabeln

Im Wilden Westen

Steffi

1 Asking questions

Was kostet	das? ein Fußball? eine Cola? ein T-Shirt?	How much is	that? a football? a coke? a T-shirt?
Was kosten	die Bonbons?	How much are the sweets?	
Kann ich hier Geld wechseln?		Can I change money here?	
Was nimmst du?		What are you having (to eat/drink)?	
Wofür gibst du dein Geld aus?		What do you spend your money on?	
Wofür sparst du dein Geld?		What are you saving up for?	
Kommst du mit zum Jahrmarkt?		Are you coming to the fair?	

Fährst du gern mit	dem	Autoscooter? Riesenrad? Karussell?	Do you like going on the	dodgems? big wheel? roundabout?
	der	Geisterbahn? Schiffschaukel?		ghost train? swing boat?

auf einen Blick

2 Changing money

Ich möchte 25 Pfund in	D-Mark Schilling Franken	umwechseln, bitte.	I'd like to change £25 into	marks, shillings, francs,	please.

3 Ordering snacks and drinks

Einmal Zweimal Dreimal	Vanille, Schokolade, Zitrone,	bitte.	One Two Three	vanilla, chocolate, lemon,	please.	

(Ich nehme) (Ich hätte gern) (Ich möchte)	einen	Hamburger, Apfelsaft,	bitte.	(I'll have) (I would like) (I would like)	a/an	hamburger, apple juice,	please.
	eine	Bratwurst, Cola, Tafel Schokolade,				fried sausage, coke, bar of chocolate,	
	ein	Schaschlik, Eis, belegtes Brot,				kebab, ice cream, open sandwich,	
	zweimal Pommes (frites),				two portions of chips,	

4 Saying what you spend your money on and what you are saving up for

Ich gebe mein Geld	für	Kleider Hobbys CDs	aus.	I spend my money	on	clothes. hobbies. CDs.
Ich spare	für	einen Computer. eine Gitarre. ein Fahrrad. neue Turnschuhe.		I'm saving up	for	a computer. a guitar. a bicycle. new trainers.

5 Saying which rides you like (most) at the fair

Ich fahre gern mit	dem	Autoscooter.	I like going on	the	dodgems.	
Am liebsten fahre ich mit	der	Achterbahn.	I like	the	big dipper	best (of all).

Lernziel 1

Wie ist das Wetter?

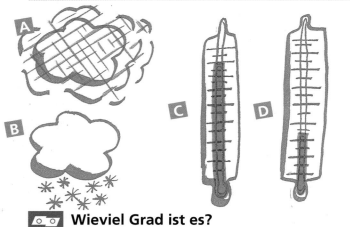

 Wieviel Grad ist es?

Sieh dir die Landkarte an, und hör zu.
Wieviel Grad ist es?

 Schönes Wetter?

Hör gut zu, und sieh dir die Bilder an.
Wie ist das Wetter?
Beispiel
1 D

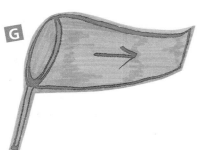

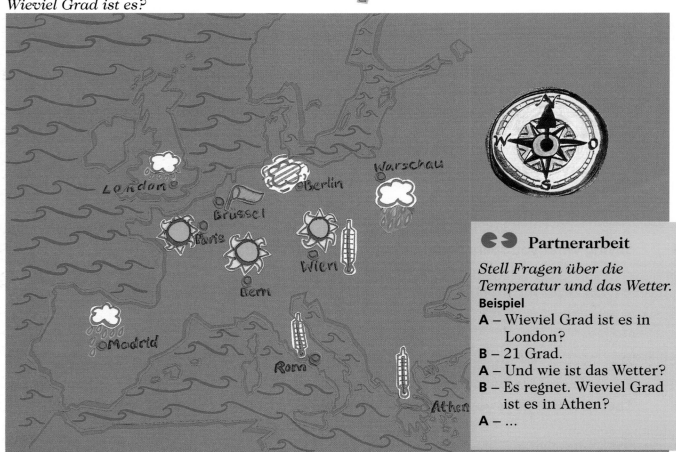

Partnerarbeit

Stell Fragen über die
Temperatur und das Wetter.
Beispiel

A – Wieviel Grad ist es in
        London?

B – 21 Grad.

A – Und wie ist das Wetter?

B – Es regnet. Wieviel Grad
        ist es in Athen?

A – ...

Ferienpostkarten

Lies diese Ferienpostkarten, und mach Notizen.

Beispiel 1

Monat? Wo? Wetter? Aktivitäten?

März Zermatt …

1

26.3.

Liebe Susi,
Es ist sehr schön hier in Zermatt. Das Wetter ist toll! Die Sonne scheint, und es schneit. Ich fahre jeden Tag ski. Abends gehe ich in die Disco.
Dein Chris

Susi Müller,
Wiesenweg 4,
53121,
Bonn

2

12.10.

Liebe Ines,
Das Wetter ist schlecht hier in Berlin. Es ist kalt, und es regnet von morgens bis abends. Ich lese viel, sehe fern und gehe oft ins kino!
Bis bald,
Dein Manfred.

Frau Ines Winter
Bahnhofstr. 60
19075 Holthusen

Jetzt bist du dran.
Schreib eine Ferienpostkarte.

3

24.7

Lieber Dieter,
wir haben tolles Wetter hier am Meer in Nizza. Es ist heiß, fast 30 Grad. Ich gehe jeden Tag schwimmen und surfen. Ich spiele auch Volleyball am Strand.
Alles Gute
Deine Frauke

Herrn
Dieter Meißner
Kapellenstraße 7
55124 MAINZ
Allemagne

Partnerarbeit.
Die Jahreszeiten in Europa

Sieh dir das Bild an. Stell Fragen.
Beispiel
A – Welche Monate sind im Herbst?
B – September, Oktober und November.
A – In welcher Jahreszeit ist Dezember?
B – Im Winter. Wie ist das Wetter meistens im Dezember?
A – Es ist kalt, und es schneit.

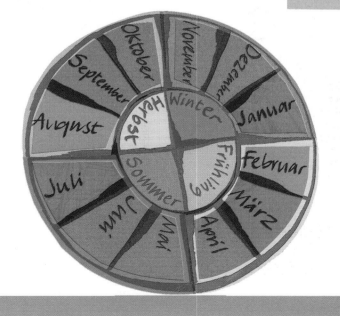

Tip des Tages

Wie ist das Wetter?				Im	Frühling. Sommer. Herbst. Winter.
Die Sonne scheint.					
	regnet. schneit.				
Es	ist	kalt. heiß. neblig. windig. schön.			

Lernziel 2
Was machst du in den Ferien?

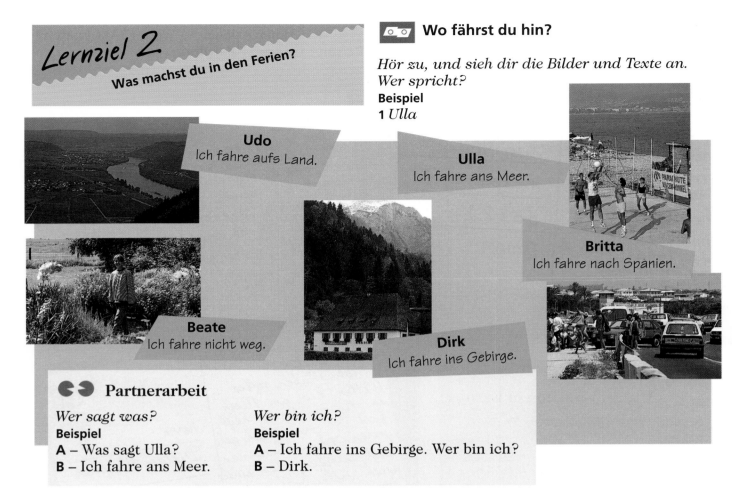

Udo
Ich fahre aufs Land.

Ulla
Ich fahre ans Meer.

Britta
Ich fahre nach Spanien.

Beate
Ich fahre nicht weg.

Dirk
Ich fahre ins Gebirge.

Wo fährst du hin?

Hör zu, und sieh dir die Bilder und Texte an.
Wer spricht?
Beispiel
1 *Ulla*

Partnerarbeit

Wer sagt was?	Wer bin ich?
Beispiel	**Beispiel**
A – Was sagt Ulla?	A – Ich fahre ins Gebirge. Wer bin ich?
B – Ich fahre ans Meer.	B – Dirk.

Partnerarbeit. Ferienpläne

Finde heraus, was für Ferienpläne dein(e) Partner(in) hat.

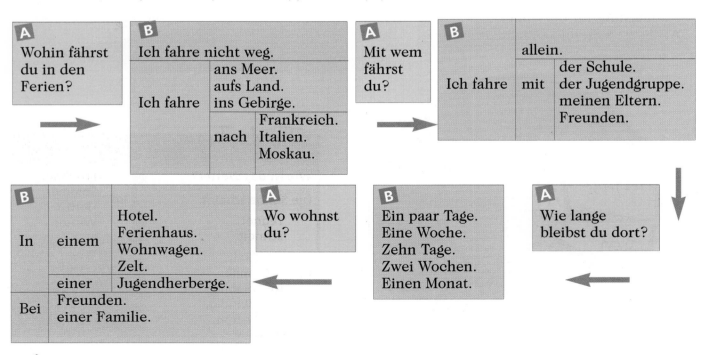

A Wohin fährst du in den Ferien? →

B
Ich fahre nicht weg.
Ich fahre ans Meer. / aufs Land. / ins Gebirge.
nach Frankreich. / Italien. / Moskau.

A Mit wem fährst du? →

B
Ich fahre allein.
Ich fahre mit der Schule. / der Jugendgruppe. / meinen Eltern. / Freunden.

A Wie lange bleibst du dort? ←

B Ein paar Tage. / Eine Woche. / Zehn Tage. / Zwei Wochen. / Einen Monat. ←

A Wo wohnst du? ←

B
In einem Hotel. / Ferienhaus. / Wohnwagen. / Zelt.
einer Jugendherberge.
Bei Freunden. / einer Familie.

Wir fahren nach Spanien ans Meer

Hör gut zu. Wer spricht? Schreib die Namen in der richtigen Reihenfolge auf.
Wohin fahren sie? Mit wem? Wie lange bleiben sie dort? Wo wohnen sie?
Schreib es in eine Tabelle.

	Name	Wohin?	Mit wem?	Wie lange?	Was für Unterkunft?
Beispiel	*Lisa*	*nach Spanien*	*Eltern + Bruder*	*14 Tage*	*Hotel*

Rudi
Ich fahre für eine Woche nach Österreich ... auf einen Campingplatz.

Kai
Ich fahre nach England.

Karola
Wir bleiben 10 Tage in verschiedenen Jugendherbergen in Dänemark.

Frauke
Ich fahre mit meinen Eltern nach Holland in ein Ferienhaus.

Gina
Ich fahre nach Mallorca ... ans Meer.

Jochen
Ich fahre nicht weg.

Lisa
Wir bleiben da 14 Tage in einem Hotel.

Rainer
Wir fahren dieses Jahr ins Gebirge.

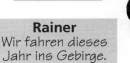

 Was paßt zusammen?

Hör gut zu, und lies die Texte.
Welches Bild paßt
zu welchem Text?
Beispiel *Gisela* **G**

Gisela
Ich fahre mit drei Freundinnen ins Gebirge. Wir übernachten in Jugendherbergen.

Ali
Ich fahre sehr gern mit meiner Familie weg. Diesen Sommer zum Beispiel fliegen wir nach Griechenland, und wir wohnen in einem Hotel.

Birgit
Dieses Jahr fahren wir auf einen Campingplatz mitten in der Natur im Schwarzwald.

Susanne
Ja, wir verbringen vierzehn Tage in einem Wohnwagen an der Ostsee. Es ist ganz schön – wir waren auch letztes Jahr dort.

Stefan
Wir fahren dieses Jahr ins Ausland und wie immer in den Süden. Warme Sonne, klares Wasser und nicht zu viele Touristen – das gefällt uns. Diesen Sommer mieten wir ein Ferienhaus in Süditalien.

Michael
Meine Schwester und ich treiben sehr gern Wintersport – meine Eltern auch – deshalb machen wir nächstes Jahr einen Winterurlaub in den Alpen.

Konstanze
Wir haben ein Ferienhaus in Süddeutschland. Da verbringen wir zwei Wochen im Juli. Mein Onkel und seine Kinder fahren auch hin.

Lernziel 3

Meint ihr uns?

🔊 Häuser und Wohnungen

Diese Jugendlichen aus Deutschland sind in Großbritannien.
Hier sind ihre Meinungen über Häuser und Wohnungen.
Hör zu. Stimmt das? Was meinst du?

> Meistens sind die Häuser klein.

> Die Häuser sehen alle gleich aus.

> Viele Engländer haben ein Haus mit Garten. In Deutschland wohne ich in einer Wohnung.

> Die Häuser sind sehr alt.

Wie ist das bei dir?

Hast du ein Haus oder eine Wohnung?
Ist dein Haus/deine Wohnung alt oder modern?
Ist dein Haus/deine Wohnung klein oder groß?
Hast du ein Haus mit Garten?
Sehen alle Häuser in deiner Straße gleich aus?

Schmeckt das?

Hör zu, und lies den Text.
Was sagen diese Leute über das
Essen in Großbritannien?

1

Bonbons, Kekse und Schokolade schmecken toll. Die Kuchen schmecken nicht so gut, finde ich.

Birgit macht einen Campingurlaub in Nordwales.

5

Ja, das Essen geht, aber ich kriege nicht genug. Nach dem Abendessen bin ich immer noch hungrig und gehe zu McDonald's.

Harald wohnt eine Woche bei einer Familie in Manchester.

2

Das Frühstück schmeckt gut, aber das Essen in der Schule ist fürchterlich! Die englischen Kuchen schmecken toll.

Jens wohnt 10 Tage bei einer Familie in Plymouth.

6

Es ist immer so ein Berg auf meinem Teller – acht Kartoffeln, dann noch Gemüse, Fleisch und Soße!

Sabine ist bei einer Familie in der Nähe von Cambridge.

3

Das Essen schmeckt immer gut. Fisch mit Pommes ist fantastisch!

Wiebke ist im Urlaub in Schottland.

7

Das Brot schmeckt mir überhaupt nicht! Der Tee schmeckt gut, aber der Kaffee ist grauenvoll!

Margit wohnt drei Wochen bei einer Familie in Birmingham.

4

Das Toastbrot zum Frühstück schmeckt mir nicht. Die Marmelade schmeckt aber gut. Die Cornflakes schmecken auch gut.

Jürgen wohnt zwei Wochen bei einer Familie in Belfast.

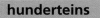

Fernsehen und Radio in Großbritannien

Hör zu, und lies den Text.
Stimmt das? Was meinst du?

In der Küche steht ein Fernseher.

Sie gucken fern zum Frühstück.

Der Fernseher ist den ganzen Tag an.

Das Radio in der Küche läuft ununterbrochen.

Sie haben ein Radio im Badezimmer.

Die Familie sitzt von sieben bis elf vor dem Fernseher.

Auch im Eßzimmer gibt es einen Fernseher.

Sie sehen fern im Bett.

Das Fernsehprogramm

Was finden die deutschen Jugendlichen gut im britischen Fernsehprogramm?
Und was finden sie nicht so gut? Schreib es auf.

Beispiel	gut	nicht so gut
	Serien	*Werbung*

Es gibt viele Musikshows.

Die Filme sind meistens amerikanisch.

Es gibt viele Komödien.

Die Serien sind gut.

Es gibt viele Tierfilme.

Die Nachrichten sind nicht so gut.

Es gibt viele Sendungen für junge Leute.

Die Nachrichten bringen wenig Informationen über Deutschland und über Europa.

Es gibt zu viel Werbung. Die kommt alle 10 Minuten.

🔊 Die Schule in Großbritannien

Hör gut zu.
Was sagen diese deutschen
Jugendlichen über die Schulen
in Großbritannien?
Stimmt das?

Der Schultag in Großbritannien											
1	2	Pause	3	4	Mittagspause	5	6	Pause	7	8

> Ich kann länger schlafen als in Deutschland.

> Der Schultag ist zu lang. Es gibt zu viele lange Pausen.

> Die Lehrer sind sehr streng. Man muß ‚Yes, Miss' oder ‚Yes, Sir' sagen.

> Der Lehrer ist der große Boß in Großbritannien.

> Sie haben zu wenig Freizeit.

> Nachmittags Schule? Ich finde das nicht gut.

> Viele kommen mit dem Schulbus zur Schule. Es gibt sehr laute Popmusik im Bus.

> Die haben samstags keine Schule. Das finde ich toll.

sb ▶ *Selbstbedienung*

Lernziel 1

Welcher Planet ist das?

Beispiel
1 *Plark*

1 Es ist kalt, und es schneit.
2 Es ist sehr kalt und neblig.
3 Es ist sehr heiß und neblig.
4 Die Sonne scheint, aber es ist sehr kalt.
5 Es ist warm, und es regnet.
6 Es ist windig und kalt.

Lernziel 1

Alles Gute!

Welcher Text paßt zu welchem Bild?

Liebe Erika,
es ist schön hier an
der Ostsee. Das
Wetter ist auch ganz
gut. Ich sitze meistens
vor dem Haus und
lese. Ich finde das
Wasser hier zu kalt
zum Schwimmen!
Bis bald!
　Dein Michael

1

Erika Rauscherbach
Springst. 2
37077 Göttingen

Liebe Bianca!
　Meine zweite Woche
hier in Spanien geht
schnell zu Ende. Das
Wetter ist fantastisch,
und der Strand ist toll.
Heute liegen wir
wieder in der Sonne.
Alles Gute!
　Deine Sabine

2

Frau
Bianca Rose
Stuttbergstraße 43
42107 WUPPERTAL

Dz 502
80/10

Lieber Werner,
　Das Wetter
hier in Bayern
ist nicht schlecht.
Nachmittags scheint
die Sonne. Wir
machen heute ein
Picknick im Wald.
Dein Ralf.

3

Werner Pabst
Bremerstr. 94
44135, Dortmund.

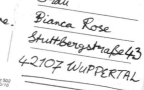

SORRENTO (NA)
Marina Grande
Grande Marine
Great Seaside
Meeresküste

Grüße aus
　Italien!

Lieber Rainer!
Hier ist es unglaublich
heiß — zu heiß, um
in der Sonne zu
liegen. Abends ist
es aber sehr kühl.
Dann gehen wir
spazieren oder in die
Disco.
　Deine Silke.

4

Rainer Falk
Barlachstr. 18
86343, Königsbrunn
Germania

Lernziel 2

 Wohin fahren sie?

Schreib die Namen und die Städte auf.
Beispiel
Brigitte – Bern

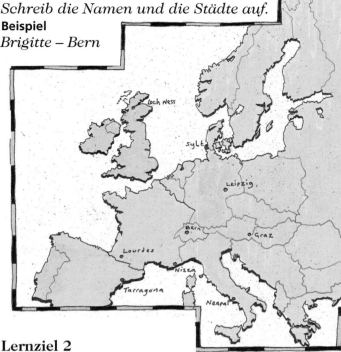

Brigitte
Ich fahre in die Schweiz.

Jürgen
Ich fahre nach Italien ans Meer.

Ulla
Ich fahre nach Frankreich ans Meer.

Petra
Ich fahre auch nach Frankreich,
aber nicht ans Meer.

Karl
Ich fahre nach Spanien ans Meer.

Werner
Ich fahre nach Norddeutschland ans Meer.

Kirsten
Ich fahre nicht weg. Ich bleibe
zu Hause in Deutschland.

Anke
Ich fahre mit der Schule nach Großbritannien.

Georg
Ich fahre nach Österreich ins Gebirge.

Lernziel 2

 Ich fahre ans Meer

Schreib die Sätze auf, und füll die Lücken aus.
Beispiel
1 *Ich fahre ans Meer.*

1 Ich fahre ans

2 Ich fahre aufs

3 Ich fahre ins

4 Ich wohne in

5 Ich bleibe 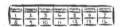 dort.

6 Ich fahre mit

Lernziel 3

 Mein Problem

Lies den Text. Was ist Michaels Problem?

Michael wohnt bei einer Familie in Coventry. Die
Familie ist sehr nett. Sie hat ein Haus in der
Stadtmitte. Es ist klein und alt. Michael kommt am
ersten Abend um neun Uhr wieder zurück zum Haus,
aber er kann das Haus nicht wiederfinden. Alle
Häuser in der Straße sehen gleich aus. Er weiß die
Hausnummer nicht, aber glücklicherweise hat er die
Telefonnummer. Er findet eine Telefonzelle und ruft
die Familie an.

Bildvokabeln

Am Strand

ein Sonnenschirm

ein Strandkorb

ein Segelboot

eine Sandburg

ein Surfbrett

ein Badetuch

eine Sonnenbrille

ein Badeanzug

die Sonnencreme

eine Luftmatratze

der Sand

Steffi

1500 Kilometer . . . Wir fahren 1500 Kilometer nach Mallorca . . .

Es kostet 7000 Mark . . .

Und worüber sprechen sie die ganze Zeit? Die Eßzimmertapete.

1 Asking questions

Wie ist das Wetter?	*What's the weather like?*
Wieviel Grad ist es in London?	*What's the temperature in London?*
Was machst du im Sommer?	*What are you doing in the summer?*
Wo fährst du hin?	*Where are you going (on holiday)?*
Wo wohnst du?	*Where are you staying?*
Wie lange bleibst du dort?	*How long are you staying there?*
Mit wem fährst du?	*Whom are you going with?*

auf einen Blick

2 Talking about the weather and the seasons

Die Sonne scheint.			*The sun is shining.*		
Es		regnet. schneit.	It is		raining. snowing.
	ist	kalt. heiß. neblig. windig. schön.			cold. hot. foggy. windy. fine.
Im		Frühling. Sommer. Herbst. Winter.	In the		spring. summer. autumn. winter.

3 Talking about holiday plans

Wir fahren		nicht weg. ans Meer. aufs Land. ins Gebirge. nach Österreich.	We're		not going away. going to the sea(side). going to the country. going to the mountains. going to Austria.
Ich fahre	mit	meinen Eltern. der Schule. einer Jugendgruppe. meiner Schwester. Freunden.	I'm going	with	my parents. school. a youth group. my sister. friends.
		alleine.			on my own.
Ich wohne	in	einem Hotel. einem Ferienhaus. einem Wohnwagen. einer Jugendherberge.	I'm staying	in	an hotel. a holiday home. a caravan. a youth hostel.
	bei	Freunden. einer Familie.		with	friends. a family.

4 Agreeing/disagreeing

Ja, das stimmt.	*Yes, that's right.*
Nein, das stimmt nicht.	*No, that's wrong.*

Wo spricht man Deutsch?

In Deutschland

Kiel
SCHLESWIG-HOLSTEIN
HAMBURG
MECKLENBURG-VORPOMMERN
Schwerin
BREMEN
NIEDERSACHSEN
BRANDENBURG
Elbe
BERLIN
Hannover
Potsdam
Weser
Magdeburg
NORDRHEIN-WESTFALEN
SACHSEN-ANHALT
Düsseldorf
Dresden
Bonn
HESSEN
Erfurt
THÜRINGEN
SACHSEN
Mosel
Wiesbaden
RHEINLAND-PFALZ
Mainz
Main
SAAR-LAND
BAYERN
Saarbrücken
In Luxemburg
Stuttgart
BADEN-WÜRTTEMBERG
Donau
Rhein
München

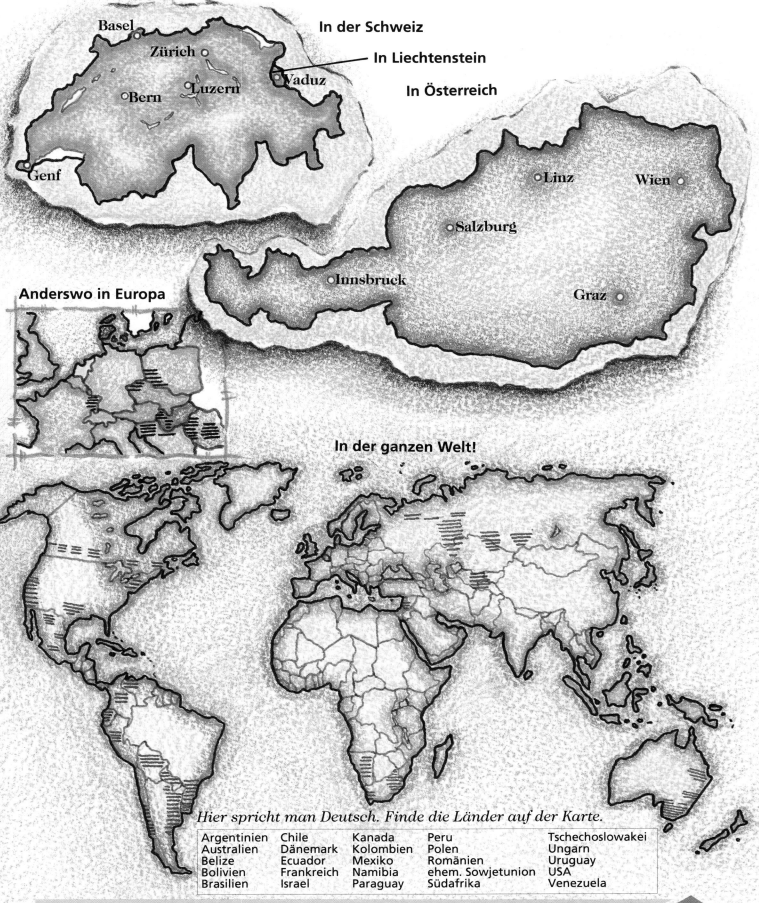

In der Schweiz

In Liechtenstein

In Österreich

Anderswo in Europa

In der ganzen Welt!

Hier spricht man Deutsch. Finde die Länder auf der Karte.

Argentinien	Chile	Kanada	Peru	Tschechoslowakei
Australien	Dänemark	Kolombien	Polen	Ungarn
Belize	Ecuador	Mexiko	Romänien	Uruguay
Bolivien	Frankreich	Namibia	ehem. Sowjetunion	USA
Brasilien	Israel	Paraguay	Südafrika	Venezuela

Spelling

1a   Capitals

All nouns begin with a capital letter (not only the words which start a sentence):

Was ißt du zum **F**rühstück? **B**rötchen und **M**armelade.	What do you eat for breakfast? Rolls and jam.

In letters **du** and its related forms are written with a capital letter:

> Liebe Christa,
>
> Was machst **D**u in den Ferien?
>
> Spielt **D**ein Bruder Tennis?
>
>   Viele Grüße,   Viele Küsse.
>
>   **D**ein Boris.   **D**eine Doris.

1b   Small letters

Adjectives are always written with small letters even if they refer to nationalities:

Ißt du gern **d**eutsches Brot? Das ist ein **e**nglisches Auto.	Do you like (eating) German bread? That's an English car.

1c   ss/ß

Use **ß** only when you are sure it is correct. If not, it is safer to write **ss**.

Use **ß**	before the letter -**t** after a long vowel at the end of a word	i**ß**t Grü**ß**e Ku**ß**	
			Viele süße Grüße und Küsse!

Numbers

2a   Cardinal numbers

1	eins	11	elf	21	einundzwanzig	100	hundert
2	zwei/zwo	12	zwölf	22	zweiundzwanzig	101	hunderteins
3	drei	13	dreizehn	29	neunundzwanzig	102	hundertzwei
4	vier	14	vierzehn	30	dreißig	199	hundertneunundneunzig
5	fünf	15	fünfzehn	40	vierzig	200	zweihundert
6	sechs	16	sechzehn	50	fünfzig	999	neunhundertneunundneunzig
7	sieben	17	siebzehn	60	sechzig		
8	acht	18	achtzehn	70	siebzig	1 000	tausend
9	neun	19	neunzehn	80	achtzig	1 000 000	eine Million
10	zehn	20	zwanzig	90	neunzig	2 000 000	zwei Millionen

2b   Ordinal numbers

These words are to say first, second, etc.
For most numbers up to **19th** you just add -**te** (or -**ten**).
Exceptions:

1st	erste(n)
3rd	dritte(n)
7th	siebte(n)
8th	achte(n)

From **20th** onwards you add-**ste** (or -**sten**).

die ers**te** Stunde; am zwanzig**ste**n März.	(See also **8a, 8b**)

Addressing people

3a Greetings

The following greetings are normally used amongst friends:

> Hallo!
> Grüß dich!
> Grüßt euch! (for more than one)
> Wie geht's?

More formal greetings are:

7.00	Guten Morgen! or Morgen!
	Guten Tag!
18.00	Guten Abend!
At mealtimes:	Guten Appetit!

3b Farewells

Tschüs!	(to friends)
(Auf) Wiedersehen!	(more formal)
(Auf) Wiederhören!	(on the telephone)
Gute Nacht, schlaf gut!	(when going to bed)

3c Ways of saying you'll see someone again

bis	eins / halb zwei / neun Uhr			at	one (o'clock) / one thirty / nine (o'clock)
bis	morgen / Samstagabend / Freitagvormittag		(I'll) see you		tomorrow / on Saturday evening / on Friday morning
	nächste	Woche		next	week
	nächsten	Monat / Samstag		next	month / Saturday
	nächstes	Jahr / Mal		next	year / time
	heute abend				this evening
	bald				soon

3d Letters

Begin	Liebe Gabi!	Dear Gabi
	Lieber Peter!	Dear Peter
End	herzliche Grüße	Best wishes
	herzliche Grüße und Küsse	Best wishes and kisses
	Schreib bald wieder!	Write again soon!
	Dein Michael	Yours, Michael
	Deine Rachel	Yours, Rachel

Questions

4a Ordinary questions

Ordinary questions can be asked in the same way as in English by beginning with the verb,
e.g. Have you ...? Do you ...? Can you ...?

Hast du Geschwister?	Have you got any brothers or sisters?
Hat sie ein Haustier?	Has she got a pet?
Ist es richtig?	Is that correct/right?
Kannst du kommen?	Can you come?

4b   Question words

Most other questions begin with a 'question word':

Wie? *(usually, how?)*	
Wie alt bist du?	*How old are you?*
Wie geht's?	*How are you?*
Wie spät ist es?	*What time is it?*
Wie ist das Wetter?	*What is the weather like?*
Wie lange arbeitest du?	*How long do you work for?*
Wie oft trinkst du Tee?	*How often do you drink tea?*

Wer? *(Who?)*	
Wer ist dein Deutschlehrer?	*Wo is your German teacher?*
Wer ist sie?	*Who is she?*
Wer bin ich?	*Who am I?*

Was? *(What?)*	
Was trinkst du gern?	*What do you like drinking?*
Was ißt du zum Frühstück?	*What do you eat for breakfast?*
Was kostet das?	*What does that cost?*

Wann? *(When?)*	
Wann hast du Geburtstag?	*When is your birthday?*
Wann kommst du?	*When are you coming?*

Wo? *(Where?)*	
Wo wohnst du?	*Where do you live?*
Wo liegt das?	*Where is that?*

Wohin? *(Where to?)*	
Wohin fährst du in den Ferien?	*Where are you going on holiday?*

Wofür? *(On what?)*	
Wofür gibst du dein Geld aus?	*What do you spend your money on?*

Wieviel? *(How many? How much?)*	
Wieviel Geschwister hast du?	*How many brothers and sisters have you got?*
Wieviel Uhr ist es?	*What time is it?*

Um wieviel Uhr? *(At what time?)*	
Um wieviel Uhr ißt du dein Mittagessen?	*When do you have lunch?*

Welche(r/s)? *(Which …?)*	
Welche Stadt ist das?	*Which town is that?*
Welches Bild ist das?	*Which picture is that?*

Days of the week

5a   What day is it?

Was ist heute für ein Tag?		*What day is it today?*	
	Montag.		*Monday.*
	Dienstag.		*Tuesday.*
	Mittwoch.		*Wednesday.*
Heute ist	Donnerstag.	*Today is*	*Thursday.*
	Freitag.		*Friday.*
	Samstag.		*Saturday.*
	Sonntag.		*Sunday.*

5b   The day and part of the day

Montag	-vormittag	*morning*
Dienstag	-nachmittag	*afternoon*
Mittwoch	-abend	*evening*

5c   On (plus the day of the week and part of the day)

am	Montag	-vormittag	*on Monday morning*
	Dienstag	-nachmittag	*on Tuesday afternoon*
	Mittwoch	-abend	*on Wednesday evening*

5d   Regularly on the same day

montags	*on Mondays*
dienstags	*on Tuesdays*
freitags	*on Fridays*

Notice that these begin with a small letter.

Months of the year

6a   die Monate

Januar	Juli
Februar	August
März	September
April	Oktober
Mai	November
Juni	Dezember

6b   In + month

Im	Januar	In	January
	Juni		June
	September		September
	Dezember		December

The seasons

7a   die Jahreszeiten

der Sommer	*summer*
der Herbst	*autumn*
der Winter	*winter*
der Frühling	*spring*

7b   In + season

Im	Sommer	In the	*summer*
	Herbst		*autumn*
	Winter		*winter*
	Frühling		*spring*

The date

8a   What's the date today?

Den wievielten haben wir heute?   What's the date today?

Wir haben den	ersten	Januar.	It's the	first of January.
	zweiten	Februar.		second of February.
	dritten	April.		third of April.
	vierten	Mai.		fourth of May.
	zehnten	Juli.		tenth of July.
	zwanzigsten	August.		twentieth of August.
	einundzwanzigsten	Oktober.		twenty-first of October.
	dreißigsten	November.		thirtieth of November.
	einunddreißigsten	Dezember.		thirty-first of December.

(See also section 2b.)

8b   On ... + date

am	ersten (1.)	Januar	on the	first of January
	dritten (3.)	Februar		third of February
	vierten (4.)	April		fourth of April
	zehnten (10.)	Juni		tenth of July
	neunzehnten (19.)	August		nineteenth of August
	zwanzigsten (20.)	November		twentieth of November

8c   Dates on letters

den	1sten	20sten	Januar
	2ten	27sten	Februar
	3ten	28sten	April
	4ten	30sten	Oktober
	18ten	31sten	Dezember

Berlin,	*den 20sten Oktober*
	den 20. Oktober

Time

9a   What time is it?

| Wieviel Uhr ist es?
Wie spät ist es? | What time is it? |

9b   On the hour

Es ist	eins. zwei. drei. vier. fünf.					It's	1 2 3 4 5	
		or	Es ist	ein zwei drei vier fünf	Uhr.			o'clock
Um	sechs.		Um	sechs		At	6	

9c   Quarter to/past the hour

Es ist	Viertel	vor	eins zwei. drei.	It's	a quarter	to	1 2
Um		nach	vier.	At		past	3 4

9d   Half past the hour

Es ist	halb	eins. zwei.	It's	half past	12 1
Um		drei.	At		2

Note: Um halb **drei** = at 2.30, i.e. halfway to 3.00.

9e   Minutes to/past the hour (5, 10, 20, 25)

Es ist	fünf zehn zwanzig	vor	eins. zwei. drei.	It's	5 10 20	to	1 2 3
Um	fünfundzwanzig	nach	vier.	At	25	past	4

Other minutes (7, 9, 14, 19 etc.)

Es ist	sieben neun vierzehn	Minuten	vor	eins. zwei. drei.	It's	7 9 14	minutes	to	1 2 3
Um	neunzehn		nach	vier.	At	19		past	4

9f   Midday/midnight

Es ist	zwölf Uhr. Mittag.	It's	12 o'clock midday
Um	Mitternacht	At	midnight

Note also the following way of saying you are doing something 'at midday/midnight':

| Zu | Mittag.
Mitternacht. |

Du, ihr, Sie

All three of these words are translated by 'you'. They are used as follows:

10a   du

Speaking to a young person

| – Wie heißt du?
– Dominik.
– Wie alt bist du?
– Acht. | What's your name?
Dominik.
How old are you?
Eight. |

Between friends old or young (people you usually call by their first name)

– Kommst du mit ins Kino? – Ja, gern.	Are you coming to the cinema? Yes, I'd like to.

In the family

– Vati, kommst du mit in die Stadt? – Nein, ich bleibe zu Hause.	Dad, are you coming into town? No, I'm staying at home.
– Kannst du mir mal helfen, Mutti? – Ja, Moment.	Can you help me, mum? Yes, wait a minute.

10b ihr

Speaking to young people

Jens – Was macht ihr heute? Alexa und Tobias – Wir gehen schwimmen.	What are you doing today? We're going swimming.
Lehrer – Was macht ihr da alle?	What are you all doing?

Speaking to friends or relatives

Ute – Mutti und Vati, geht ihr heute abend ins Kino?	Mum and dad, are you going to the cinema tonight?
Paul – Oma, Opa, kommt ihr zu meinem Geburtstag?	Grandma and grandpa, are you coming to my birthday?

10c Sie

Talking to one or more adults (other than close friends or relatives)

– Wo wohnen Sie? – Wie heißen Sie?	Where do you live? What's your name?

Verbs

11a The infinitive

In the vocabulary list, verbs are listed in the **infinitive**.
The infinitive ending is **-en**.
This is the part of the word which means 'to', for example 'to eat', 'to do', etc.

wohn**en** heiß**en** ess**en**	**to** live **to** be called **to** eat

(See also sections **11n**, **11o**, and **18c**.)

11b Present Tense (regular verbs)

Verbs which follow the usual pattern are called **regular verbs**.

11c Talking about yourself (I): ich

The verb ending that goes with **ich** is **-e**:

Ich heiß**e** Kurt Meier. **Ich** wohn**e** in München.	My name is … I live in …

(For **ich bin**, **ich muß**, **ich will** etc. see section **11j - n**.)

11d Talking to other people (you)

Address one friend or young person as du

The verb ending that goes with **du** is **-st**:

Wo wohn**st du**? Was mein**st du**?	Where do you live? What do you mean?

Verbs with an s-sound before endings just add a **-t**:

Wie heiß**t du**?	What's your name?
Was lies**t du**?	What are you reading?

Address more than one friend or young people as ihr

The verb ending that goes with **ihr** *is* **-t:**

Wo wohn**t ihr**?	Where do you live?
Was eß**t ihr**?	What are you eating?

Address one or more adults as Sie

(**Sie** *with a capital S!*)
The verb ending that goes with **Sie** *is* -**en:**

Wo wohn**en Sie**?	Where do you live?
Wie heiß**en Sie**?	What is your name?

11e Talking about somebody or something (he/she/it/one): er/sie/es/man

The verb ending that goes with **er/sie/es/man,** *or with a name, is* **-t:**

Mein Onkel wohn**t** in Wien.	My uncle lives in …
Er heiß**t** Kurt.	His name is …
Frau Meier wohn**t** in Österreich.	Mrs Meier lives in …
Sie heiß**t** Erika.	Her name is …
Mein Meerschweinchen heiß**t** Amanda.	My guinea pig is called Amanda.
Es trink**t** Milch.	It drinks milk.
In Österreich sprich**t man** Deutsch.	They speak German in Austria.

11f Talking about yourself and others (we): wir

The verb ending that goes with **wir** *is* -**en:**

Wir wohn**en** in Köln.	We live in Cologne.
Wir ess**en** Brot mit Wurst.	We eat bread with sausage.
Meine Schwester und ich trink**en** Kaffee.	My sister and I drink coffee.

11g Talking about others or things (they): sie

(**Sie** *with a small s!*)
The ending that goes with **sie** *is* -**en:**

Die Häuser steh**en** am Stadtrand.	The houses are on the outskirts of town.
Sie steh**en** am Stadtrand.	They are on the outskirts of town.
Die Meiers wohn**en** in Österreich.	The Meiers live in Austria.
Die Jungen heiß**en** Peter und Michael.	The boys are called Peter and Michael.
Sie trink**en** Milch.	They drink milk.

11h Regular verb endings at a glance

Look again at sections **11b - 11g.** *Here is the complete pattern of endings for regular verbs:*

Infinitive: **wohn en** *(**to** live)*

ich	-e	Ich **wohne** in Hamburg.	I live/am living in Hamburg.
du	-st	**Wohnst** du in Berlin?	Do you live in Berlin?
er			
sie			
es	-t	Sie **wohnt** hier.	She lives here.
man			
wir	-en	Wir **wohnen** in Leeds.	We live/are living in Leeds.
ihr	-t	**Wohnt** ihr in Deutschland?	Do you live in Germany?
Sie	-en	**Wohnen** Sie in der Schweiz?	Do you live in Switzerland?
sie	-en	Sie **wohnen** in der Stadmitte.	They live in the town centre.

Note:	Sie	=	*you*
	sie	=	*they*

11i   Irregular changes affecting some verbs

Sometimes the main vowel in the infinitive changes, but only affects the **du** *and* **er/sie/es** *parts of the verb:*

essen	du **i**ßt er **i**ßt	**e - i**	*you eat* *he eats*
sprechen	du spr**i**chst man spr**i**cht		*you speak* *one speaks/they speak*
lesen	du l**ie**st sie l**ie**st	**e - ie**	*you read* *she reads*
sehen	du s**ie**hst er s**ie**ht		*you see* *he sees*
schlafen	du schl**ä**fst er schl**ä**ft	**a - ä**	*you sleep* *he sleeps*
tragen	du tr**ä**gst sie tr**ä**gt		*you wear* *she wears*

11j   Some special verbs

Some very common verbs, which are used very frequently, are irregular
(i.e. they don't follow the normal pattern), and should be learnt separately.

11k   haben (to have)   *Just two forms are not regular:*

| **Hast** du ein Haustier?
Tante Liesel **hat** ein Reihenhaus. | | du   **hast** …
er/sie/es **hat** … | *you have* …
he/she/it has … |

11l   sein (to be)   *All the parts of this verb are irregular:*

| **Ich bin** 13 Jahre alt.
Wer **bist du**?
Er ist 15 Jahre alt.
Sie ist sehr groß.
Es ist schön hier.
Man ist Deutscher.
Maria und ich sind Geschwister.
Seid ihr alle da?
Wer **sind Sie**?
Veronica und Kirsten sind in der Schule. | ich   **bin**
du   **bist**
er
sie } **ist**
es
man
wir   **sind**
ihr   **seid**
Sie   **sind**
sie   **sind** | *I am*
you are
he is
she is
it is
one is/they are/you are
we are
you are
you are
they are |

11m   wissen (to know)   *Three parts of this verb are irregular:*

| **Ich weiß** nicht.
Weißt du das?
Sie weiß nicht. | *I don't know.*
Do you know that?
She doesn't know. | ich   **weiß**
du   **weißt**
er/sie/es **weiß** | *I know*
you know
he/she/it knows |

11n   Modal verbs

This is the name given to the following group of verbs:

	können (can)	**müssen** (must, have to)	**wollen** (want to)	**sollen** (should)	**dürfen** (allowed to)
ich	kann	muß	will	soll	darf
du	kannst	mußt	willst	sollst	darfst
er/sie/es/man	kann	muß	will	soll	darf
wir	können	müssen	wollen	sollen	dürfen
ihr	könnt	müßt	wollt	sollt	dürft
Sie	können	müssen	wollen	sollen	dürfen
sie	können	müssen	wollen	sollen	dürfen

These verbs usually lead to **another verb**, *at the end of the clause, which is in the infinitive:*

| **Willst** du **mitkommen**?
Ich **muß** hier **bleiben.** | *Do you* **want to come along**?
I **have to stay** *here.* |

Note that there is no need to write **zu** *before the verbs which follow modal verbs, unlike in the following section.*

11o   Zu + an infinitive

The infinitive of a verb means 'to …' , but sometimes an extra **zu** appears before it:

Was gibt es in der Stadt **zu sehen**?	What is there **to see** in the town?
Noch etwas **zu trinken**?	Anything else **to drink**?
Hast du Lust, Tennis **zu spielen**?	Would you like **to play** tennis?

11p   Commands

There are three main ways of giving commands in German:

Talking to a friend, or the teacher talking to one student	Talking to two or more friends, or the teacher talking to two or more students	Talking to adults, teachers, officials, shopkeepers	
Komm 'rein.	Kommt 'rein.	Kommen Sie herein.	Come in.
Setz dich.	Setzt euch.	Setzen Sie sich.	Sit down.
Schlag das Buch auf.	Schlagt das Buch auf.	Schlagen Sie das Buch auf.	Open the book.
Hör gut zu.	Hört gut zu.	Hören Sie gut zu.	Listen carefully.
Mach weiter.	Macht weiter.	Machen Sie weiter.	Continue working now.
Schreib es auf.	Schreibt es auf.	Schreiben Sie es auf.	Write it down.
Trag die Tabelle ein.	Tragt die Tabelle ein.	Tragen Sie die Tabelle ein.	Copy the chart.
Lies die Namen.	Lest die Namen.	Lesen Sie die Namen.	Read the names.
Schau auf die Karte.	Schaut auf die Karte.	Schauen Sie auf die Karte.	Look at the map.
Füll die Lücken aus.	Füllt die Lücken aus.	Füllen Sie die Lücken aus.	Fill in the gaps.

Note that sometimes these may be followed by an exclamation mark, e.g. **Komm 'rein!**

11q   Reflexive verbs

These verbs require an extra (reflexive) pronoun, and are called 'reflexive' because the action 'reflects back' on the doer:

Ich wasche **mich** um sieben Uhr.	I have a wash at 7.00. (i.e. **I** wash **myself** …)

11r   Separable verbs

Some verbs include a prefix, which separates from the main part of the verb and is placed at the end of the clause.
Some examples of separable verbs are **auf**stehen, **aus**fallen, **fern**sehen.

Ich **stehe** um halb sieben **auf**.	I get up at half past six.
Die erste Stunde **fällt aus**.	The first lesson is being cancelled.
Ich **sehe** gern **fern**.	I like watching TV.

11s   The Future Tense

The simplest way of talking about the future in German is to use the Present Tense of the verb with a word or phrase to indicate the future:

Time marker	Present Tense	
Morgen	**fahre ich** nach Frankfurt.	Tomorrow I'm going to Frankfurt.
Nächste Woche	**gehe ich** schwimmen.	I'm going swimming next week.
Am Montag	**besuche ich** meine Großeltern.	I'm visiting my grandparents on Monday.
Dieses Jahr	**fahren wir** auf einen Campingplatz.	We're going to a campsite this year.

Negatives

12a   kein

kein (no, not a) **is used before a noun.** It changes its endings like **ein**. (See section **14**):

Ich habe	**keinen** Hund.	I haven't got a dog.
Hast du	**keine** Katze?	Have you got a cat?
Sie hat	**kein** Haustier.	She has no pets.
Sie haben	**keine** Geschwister.	They have no brothers and sisters.

12b   nicht

nicht (not) **is used in other situations:**

Ich spiele **nicht** gern Tennis.	I don't like playing tennis.
Ich esse **nicht** gern Schokolade.	I don't like eating chocolate.
Er kommt **nicht** mit ins Kino.	He isn't coming with us to the cinema.
Sie geht **nicht** in die Stadt.	She isn't going into town.

12c   nichts

nichts (nothing/not anything)

| Ich trinke **nichts** zum Frühstück. | I don't drink anything for breakfast. |

Nouns

13a   Writing nouns

Remember that nouns are **always** written with a capital letter.

13b   Genders: The three groups of nouns

M	F	N
der Hund	**die** Katze	**das** Pferd
(the dog)	(the cat)	(the horse)

English has one article (one word for 'the') for all nouns, but German nouns have either **der**, **die** or **das**. These are called 'masculine' (**M**), 'feminine' (**F**) and 'neuter' (**N**).

Note also the words for 'a':

M	F	N
ein Hund	**eine** Katze	**ein** Pferd
(a dog)	(a cat)	(a horse)

13c   Plurals: Talking about more than one person, thing etc.

Nouns change in various ways in the plural, but **der**, **die**, **das** all become **die**:

SINGULAR	der	die	das
PLURAL		**die**	

The plurals are usually shown in the vocabulary list in the following way:

der	Hund(e)	**(e)**	means that the plural is (die) Hund**e**
die	Katze(n)	**(n)**	means that the plural is (die) Katze**n**
das	Haus(¨er)	**(¨er)**	means that the plural is (die) H**ä**us**er**
das	Zimmer(–)	**(–)**	means that the plural stays the same: (die) Zimmer

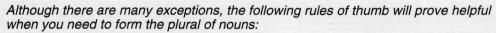

Although there are many exceptions, the following rules of thumb will prove helpful when you need to form the plural of nouns:

Many masculine plural nouns end in -e:

Hund	*dog*	Hund**e**	*dogs*
Freund	*friend*	Freund**e**	*friends*

Many neuter plural nouns end in -e or ¨-er:

Heft	*exercise book*	Heft**e**	*exercise books*
Haus	*house*	Häus**er**	*houses*

A large number of feminine plural nouns end in -n or -en:

Katze	*cat*	Katz**en**	*cats*
Straße	*street*	Straß**en**	*streets*
Schwester	*sister*	Schwester**n**	*sisters*
Wohnung	*flat*	Wohnung**en**	*flats*

13d   Some nouns have different masculine and feminine forms:

M	F	
Arzt	Ärztin	*doctor*
Freund	Freundin	*friend*
Partner	Partnerin	*partner*
Sänger	Sängerin	*singer*
Schüler	Schülerin	*pupil*
Student	Studentin	*student*
Verkäufer	Verkäuferin	*sales assistant*

13e   Nationalities

There are different masculine and feminine forms here, too:

M		F	
Engländer	*English man*	Engländerin	*English woman*
Österreicher	*Austrian man*	Österreicherin	*Austrian woman*
Schweizer	*Swiss man*	Schweizerin	*Swiss woman*
Italiener	*Italian man*	Italienerin	*Italian woman*
Deutscher	*German man*	Deutsche	*German woman*
Ire	*Irish man*	Irin	*Irish woman*
Schotte	*Scottish man*	Schottin	*Scottish woman*
Franzose	*French man*	Französin	*French woman*

13f   Compound nouns

Sometimes two (or more) nouns join together to form a new noun, called a compound noun. The gender (M, F or N) is decided by the second (or last) noun:

Stadt + **der** Plan	**der** Stadtplan	*street plan*
Haupt + **die** Post	**die** Hauptpost	*main post office*
Kranken + **das** Haus	**das** Krankenhaus	*hospital*
Jahr + **der** Markt	**der** Jahrmarkt	*fair*
Fuß + Gänger + **die** Zone	**die** Fußgängerzone	*pedestrian precinct*

Note how compound nouns, like all other nouns, have only one capital letter.

Cases

14a   The Cases

When articles (words for 'the' and 'and') change, nouns are said to be in different cases. You can see from the illustrations here how important it can be to put articles in the correct cases!

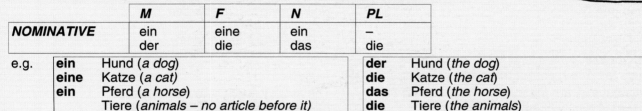

| – Was, die Katze frißt **den** Wellensittich? – Nein, **der** Hund. | What, the cat is eating the budgie? No, the dog (is eating the budgie). |
| – Was, die Katze frißt **den** Wellensittich? – Nein, **den** Goldfisch. | What, the cat is eating the budgie? No, (the cat is eating) the goldfish. |

14b   The Nominative case

In dictionaries and glossaries nouns always appear in the **Nominative case.**

	M	F	N	PL
NOMINATIVE	ein der	eine die	ein das	– die

e.g.

ein Hund (*a dog*)	**der** Hund (*the dog*)
eine Katze (*a cat*)	**die** Katze (*the cat*)
ein Pferd (*a horse*)	**das** Pferd (*the horse*)
Tiere (*animals – no article before it*)	**die** Tiere (*the animals*)

The Nominative case is used for the **subject** of the sentence.

14c   The Accusative case

In the **Accusative case** articles change as follows:

	M	F	N	PL
ACCUSATIVE	**einen** **den**	eine die	ein das	– die

As you can see, the **only difference** between the Nominative and Accusative is that **ein (M)** changes to **einen** and that **der** changes to **den**.

The Accusative case is used for the direct object of the sentence.

Look at this rhyme – it might be useful to learn it off by heart to help you remember the Accusative case.

NOMINATIVE	VERB	ACCUSATIVE	
Frau Bamster	hat	**einen** Hamster.	M
Klaus	hat	**eine** Maus.	F
Gerd	hat	**ein** Pferd.	N
Sabinchen	hat	zwölf Kaninchen	PL

14d   Es gibt

This phrase is followed by the Accusative case and means 'there is/there are …'

| **Es gibt** einen Marktplatz in der Stadtmitte. | There is a market place in the town centre. |
| **Es gibt** dreißig Schüler in der Klasse 7b. | **There are** thirty pupils in Class 7b. |

14e   The Dative case

In the **Dative case** articles change even more, as follows:

	M	F	N	PL
DATIVE	**einem** **dem**	**einer** **der**	**einem** **dem**	– **den**

Note: all nouns in the Dative plural add an **-n** whenever possible:

(die Berge)	in den Berge**n**	*in the mountains*
(die Häuser)	in den Häuser**n**	*in the houses*
(die Freunde)	bei Freunde**n**	*(staying) with friends*

but

| (die Hotels) | in den Hotels | *in the hotels* |

Prepositions

15a   Prepositions

Prepositions are words like 'in', 'on', 'under', 'through', 'by', 'for', etc.
In German all prepositions must be followed by particular cases.

15b   Some prepositions which are sometimes followed by the Accusative case, and sometimes by the Dative case

Here are some prepositions which are followed by either the Accusative, or the Dative case, depending on whether movement is involved:

an	to; by; on	auf	onto; on	in	into; in

*The **Accusative case** is used after these prepositions*
*when there is **movement to or away from** the place mentioned:*

Wir fahren **an die** See.	We're going to the seaside.
Er geht **auf den** Balkon.	He's going onto the balcony.
Sie geht **in den** Garten.	She's going into the garden.
Ich gehe **in die** Stadt.	I'm going into town.
Er kommt **ins** Zimmer.	He's coming into the room.

*The **Dative case** is used after these prepositions*
*when there is **no movement to or away from** the place mentioned:*

Das Ferienhaus ist **am** Meer.	The holiday home is by the sea.
Klaus ißt sein Frühstück **auf dem** Balkon.	Klaus eats his breakfast on the balcony.
Ich bin **in der** Stadt.	I'm in the town.
Er sitzt **im Auto.**	He's sitting in the car.

Note also: im Norden

im Westen   ⊕   im Osten   in Nordostengland

im Süden   in Südwestengland

15c   Some prepositions which are always followed by the Accusative

*Here are some prepositions which must always be followed by the **Accusative case**:*

durch	through	für	for	um	round

Ich fahre **durch die** Stadt.	I drive through the town.
Das ist **für meinen** Bruder.	That's for my brother.
Sie geht **um die** Ecke.	She goes round the corner.

15d   Some prepositions which are always followed by the Dative

*Here are some prepositions which must always be followed by the **Dative case**:*

aus	out of; from	mit	with	von	from; of
bei	at (the home of)	nach	after	zu	to

Er kommt **aus der** Schweiz.	He comes from Switzerland.
Bei mir zu Hause.	At my house.
Ich treffe mich **mit meinen** Freunden.	I meet my friends.
Nach dem Mittagessen spiele ich Tennis.	After lunch I'm going to play tennis.
Sie wohnt nicht weit **von der** Stadtmitte.	She doesn't live far from the town centre.
Er fährt mit dem Rad **zur** Schule	I go to school by bike.
Was ißt du **zum** Frühstück?	What do you eat for breakfast?

15e   Contracted prepositions

Sometimes the preposition and article are combined:

am an dem	**im** in dem	**zum** zu dem	**beim** bei dem
ans an das	**ins** in das	**zur** zu der	

15f   Countries

Use **nach** when talking about going to most countries (+ towns and villages):

Ich fahre	**nach**	Italien/Spanien/Polen/Frankreich/Schottland/Nordirland. Berlin/München/Wien.
I'm going	to	Italy/Spain/Poland/France/Scotland/Northern Ireland. Berlin/Munich/Vienna.

But use **in die** with this country:

Ich fahre	**in die**	Schweiz.
I'm going	to	Switzerland.

Pronouns

16a   Pronouns

These are words like 'she', 'they', 'him', 'it' in English, which can replace nouns.

16b   Nominative case pronouns

ich	I	**Ich** spiele gern Fußball.	**I** like playing football
du	you	Wie alt bist **du**?	How old are **you**?
er	he	**Er** (= der Hund) heißt Rowdy.	**He** (the dog) is called Rowdy.
sie	she	**Er** (= der Wagen) ist rot.	**It*** (the car) is red.
es	it	**Sie** (= die Katze) heißt Mitzi.	**She** (the cat) is called Mitzi.
wir	we	**Es** (= das Pferd) heißt Rex.	**He*** (the horse) is called Rex.
ihr	you	**Wir** gehen in die Stadt.	**We** are going to town.
Sie	you (polite)	Habt **ihr** Geld dabei?	Have **you** got any money with you?
sie	they	Wie heißen **Sie**?	What are **you** called?
		Sie trinken gern Cola.	**They** like drinking coke.

***es** in German can sometimes be 'he' or 'she' in English, just as **er** and **sie** can mean 'it'.

16c   Accusative case pronouns

ich	**mich**	me	Ist das für **mich**? Oh, wie schön!	Is that for **me**? How nice!
du	**dich**	you	Hier ist ein Geschenk für **dich**.	Here is a present for **you**.
er	**ihn**	him		
sie	**sie**	her	Ich finde **sie** sehr schick.	I think **it's** very smart.
es	**es**	it		
wir	**uns**	us		
ihr	**euch**	you		
Sie	**Sie**	you (polite)	Das ist für **Sie**, Frau Schmidt.	This is for **you**, Mrs Schmidt.
sie	**sie**	them		

16d   Dative case pronouns

ich	**mir**	me, to me	Er wohnt bei **mir**.	He lives at **my house**.
du	**dir**	you, to you		
er	**ihm**	him, to him	Es geht **ihm** gut.	**He** is fine.
sie	**ihr**	her, to her	Wie geht's **ihr**?	How is **she**?
es	**ihm**	it, to it		
wir	**uns**	us, to us	**Uns** ist zu warm.	**We** are too warm.
ihr	**euch**	you, to you		
Sie	**Ihnen**	you, to you	Kann ich **Ihnen** helfen?	Can I help **you**?
sie	**ihnen**	them, to them		

16e   Some special verbs requiring Dative pronouns

gefallen	
Das gefällt **mir** gut.	I like that.
Wie gefällt **dir** mein Pullover?	What do you think of my pullover?
schmecken	
Wie schmeckt **dir** der Kuchen?	Do you like the cake?
Schmeckt es **dir**?	Do you like it?
gehen (meaning how someone is)	
Es geht **mir** gut, danke.	I'm fine, thank you.

Adjectives

17a   Adjectives

Adjectives are words which describe nouns. They have no endings in sentences like this:

Jürgen ist **toll**. Jürgen is great.	Annette ist **nett**. Annette is nice.	Das ist **billig**. That's cheap.

17b   Adjectival agreement

When adjectives are used next to a noun they have different endings. These depend on the gender and case of the noun, whether it is singular or plural and any other word which is used before it. This is called adjectival agreement and will be explained at a later stage, but here are some examples you have met already:

In der Stadtmitte steht ein alt**er** Mann, alt**e** Schuhe und ein alt**er** Hut.	In der erst**en** Stunde ...

17c   Mein, dein, sein (possessive adjectives) and kein

Mein, **dein**, **sein** and **kein** follow this pattern:

	M	F	N	PL
NOMINATIVE	mein	meine	mein	meine
ACCUSATIVE	meinen	meine	mein	meine
DATIVE	meinem	meiner	meinem	meinen

In the singular, the pattern is the same as **ein**, **eine**, **ein**.

Dies ist **mein** Vater.	This is my father.	Ist das **deine** Mutter?	Is that your mother?
Er hat **keinen** Hund.	He doesn't have a dog.	Hast du **keine** Katze?	Haven't you got a cat?
Du hast **mein** Heft!	You've got my book!	Sie hat **seinen** Bleistift.	She has his pencil.
Das ist in **meinem** Heft.	That is in my exercise book.	Er ist mit **meiner** Mutter.	He is with my mother.

Ihr (her), **euer** (your) and **unser** (our) also follow the same pattern.

Word order

18a   Word order

There are various rules in German governing where words should be placed in a sentence.

18b   Main clauses

Most of the sentences in this book are called **main clauses**.
Except when asking questions like **Hast du ...?**, **Kommst du ...?** (see section 4), the verb is always the second piece of information:

1	2 (VERB)	3	
Ich	heiße	Peter.	I'm called Peter.
Mein Name	ist	Krull.	My name is Krull.
Wie	heißt	du?	What are you called?
Um wieviel Uhr	ißt	du dein Mittagessen?	When do you eat lunch?
Dann	gehe	ich zur Schule.	Then I go to school.
Einige Minuten später	kommt	Anna ins Zimmer.	A few minutes later Anna comes into the room.

18c   Sentences with more than one verb

When there are two verbs in a sentence, the second verb is usually in the **infinitive**.
(See sections **11n** and **11o**.)

The infinitive is **at the end of the sentence:**

	FIRST VERB		**INFINITIVE**	
Ich	gehe	gern	**schwimmen**.	I like going swimming.
Wo	kann	ich Postkarten	**kaufen**?	Where can I buy postcards?
Du	kannst	zu uns	**kommen**.	You can come to our house.
Was	willst	du	**sehen**?	What do you want to see?

18d   When? How? Where? in the same sentence.

In a German sentence, if two or more of these elements are present, they should come in this order:

1 **When? (Time)**	2 **How? (Manner)**	3 **Where? (Place)**

If a time and a place are mentioned, the **time** comes before the **place:**

TIME		**PLACE**	
Nächste Woche	fahre ich	**nach München**.	Next week I'm going to Munich.

or

	TIME	**PLACE**	
Ich fahre	**nächste Woche**	**nach München**.	Next week I'm going to Munich.

If you say **how** you are going somewhere, this must come **before** the **place:**

	MANNER	**PLACE**	
Ich fahre	**mit dem Bus**	**zum Schwimmbad**.	I'm going to the swimming pool by bus.

If you say **when, how** and **where** you are going, they must go in that order:

	TIME	**MANNER**	**PLACE**	
Ich fahre	**nächste Woche**	**mit dem Zug**	**nach Köln**.	Next week, I'm going to Cologne by train.

Likes and favourites

19a   Talking about what you like doing

Gern can be used with most verbs to show that you **like** doing something:

Ich trinke Kaffee.	I drink coffee.
Ich trinke **gern** Kaffee.	I **like** drinking coffee.
Ich gehe schwimmen.	I go swimming.
Ich gehe **gern** schwimmen.	I **like** going swimming.

Notice how you say that you like **something** (a noun):

Ich **habe** Katzen **gern**.	I **like** cats.
Ich **habe** Tee **gern**.	I **like** tea.

19b   Talking about what you like doing most of all

Start the sentence with **am liebsten**, and remember that the next thing must be a verb:

Am liebsten spiele ich Fußball.	I **like** playing football **most of all**.
Am liebsten gehe ich schwimmen.	I **like** going swimming **most of all**.

Note also the use of **Lieblings-** with a noun:

Fußball ist mein **Lieblingssport**.	Football is my **favourite** sport.
Mein **Lieblingsfach** ist Deutsch.	My **favourite** lesson is German.

Using a dictionary

To help you find the German equivalents of English words, and vice versa, you will need to use a bilingual German-English dictionary, that is one which is divided into two halves: German-English, and English-German. Hence if you come across a German word and need to find its English meaning, you should look it up in the German-English half of your dictionary. If you want to find the German for an English word, use the English-German section.

German-English

1 **Looking up the meaning of a German word**

Will the word you are looking up be in the dictionary?
- *It may not be if it is the name of a place or a person. (It's not so easy to recognise these in German, since all nouns have capital letters.)*
- *It may be there, but with a different ending.*

Adjectives are normally listed without endings:

nächstes Jahr	*look up* **nächst**
am **dritten** Mai	*look up* **dritt**

Nouns are normally listed in the singular:

in den **Bergen**	*look up* **Berg**
Die **Häuser** sind groß.	*look up* **Haus**

Verbs are normally listed in the infinitive:

Ich **besuche** meine Großeltern.	*look up* **besuchen**
Schreib es auf.	*look up* **schreiben**
Ich habe im Bus **geschlafen**.	*look up* **schlafen**

2 **Looking up the meaning of a phrase**

When you encounter a phrase which you don't understand, begin by looking up the meaning of the noun(s), i.e. the words beginning with capital letters:

zum Frühstück	*look up* **Frühstück**
auf Wiedersehen	*look up* **Wiedersehen**
in der Nähe von München	*look up* **Nähe** (*not* **München**, *because that is a proper name*)

3 **Looking up compound nouns (two nouns joined together to make another word)**

Look up the first noun – other nouns that can be joined to it will be listed alphabetically in the paragraph that follows:

e.g. **Bratkartoffeln** *look up* **Brat-**, *then look in the examples for* **-kartoffeln**, *as here:*

> **Brat-:** ~**fett das** (cooking) fat; ~**fisch der** fried fish; ~**hähnchen das**, *(südd., österr.)* ~**hendl das** roast chicken; *(gegrillt)* broiled chicken; ~**hering der** fried herring; ~**kartoffeln** *Pl.* fried potatoes; home fries *(Amer.)*; ~**pfanne die** frying-pan; ~**spieß der** spit; ~**wurst die** (fried/grilled) sausage

(Extract from **The Pocket Oxford-Duden German Dictionary***, Oxford University Press)*

4 **What else the dictionary tells you about nouns**

As well as telling you the English meaning of a noun you are looking up, a dictionary includes two other important pieces of information:
- *its gender (der, die or das – masculine, feminine or neuter);*
- *its plural form.*

e.g. | **Kind das; -[e]s, -er a)** child |

(Extract from **The Pocket Oxford-Duden German Dictionary***, Oxford University Press)*

This tells you
- *that the word* **Kind** *is neuter, i.e. it's* **das Kind**.
- *that the plural (the German for 'children') is* **Kinder**.

English-German

There is so much information in a dictionary, it's easy to make a mistake. So take the following precautions when you look up the German for an English word.

a If it's a noun you are looking for, make sure the German has a capital letter. Some dictionaries put the letter **n** after the word to show it's a noun. Don't forget to see whether it's der, die or das and to see how it forms its plural.

b If it's a verb you are looking for, check that it has the letter **V** after it. If it also has **ir.** or **unr.** after it, this means that the verb is irregular (unregelmäßig), in other words that there are spelling changes in some parts of the verb. Check in the grammar section of your book where such changes occur. Some dictionaries also include a list of irregular verbs with their modifications.

c If you can't find the word you are looking for, ask yourself whether it might be listed under something else. Is it a part of a verb? Is it a plural noun that should be looked up in the singular?
For example:

am	look up **be**
slept	look up **sleep**
gone	look up **go**
mice	look up **mouse**

Some dictionaries will list these words anyway and will tell you where to look them up.

d Double checking. Whatever you are looking up, it's wise to make sure you have found the right word by looking up the German in the other half of the dictionary.

If you want to find out the German for **to fish**, for example, look up **fish** in the English-German half (remembering to look for the verb, V, and not the noun!). You will find the word **angeln**. Then turn to the German-English half and look up **angeln** there. If it says **fish**, you know you've got the right word.

Remember, the more you use a dictionary, the more familiar you will become with the way a language works and you will be able to find the correct words more easily.

The **ZICKZACK neu** Stage 1 Copymasters also provide activities to help you practise using a dictionary. Ask your teacher for a worksheet.

A

der **Abend(e)** evening
das **Abendbrot(-)** supper, evening meal
das **Abendessen(-)** evening meal
das **Abenteuer(-)** adventure
der **Absender(-)** sender
acht eight
achtzehn eighteen
achtzig eighty
die **Achterbahn(en)** big dipper
die **Adresse(n)** address
die **Aktivität(en)** activity
alle(r/s) all
alles everything
alles Gute! all the best!
allein alone
der **Alltag(e)** weekday
die **Alpen** the Alps
das **Alphabet** alphabet
das **Alphabetlied** alphabet song
das **Alphaberätsel(-)** alphabet puzzle
als than, as; when (past)
alt old
ich bin 13 Jahre alt I'm 13 years old
der **Altbau** old building
der **Alte(n)** old man
Amerika America
amerikanisch American
an (+ Acc/Dat) to, on, at
an/fangen to begin
an/passen to fit, be suitable
an/rufen to telephone
an/sehen to look at
andere(r/s) other (one)
anders (als) different (from)
anderthalb one and a half
der **Anfang(¨e)** beginning
am Anfang April at the beginning of April
anonym anonymously
die **Antwort(en)** answer
die **Anzeige(n)** display, notice
der **Anzug(¨e)** suit
der **Apfel(¨)** apple
der **Apfelsaft** apple juice
April April
arbeiten to work
die Partnerarbeit pairwork
der **Arbeitstag** working day
arm poor
Athen Athens
der **Athlet(en)** athlete
auch also, too
auf on, onto
auf deutsch in German
auf einen Blick at a glance
die **Auferstehung** resurrection
auf/schreiben to write down
auf/stehen to get up, stand up
steh auf! get up, stand up
auf/wachen to wake up
aufrecht upright
August August

die **Aula (Aulen)** assembly hall
aus out, out of
aus/geben to spend (money)
aus/gehen to go out
das **Ausland** abroad
die **Ausrede(n)** excuse
eine gute Ausrede a good excuse
aus/sehen to look like
Australien Australia
um **auszutreiben** to drive away (evil spirits)
das **Auto** car
20 Autominuten von Hamburg 20 minutes by car from Hamburg
der **Autoscooter(-)** dodgems

B

das **Baby(s)** baby
das **Babyfoto(s)** baby photos
backen to bake, cook
die **Bäckerei(en)** baker's
das **Bad(¨er)** bath, bathing
der **Badeanzug(¨e)** bathing suit
das **Badetuch(¨er)** bath towel
die **Badewanne** bath(tub)
das **Badezimmer(-)** bathroom
der **Balkon(s)** balcony
die **Banane(n)** banana
Basketball basketball
beantworten to answer
beginnen to begin
der **Beginn** beginning
bei (+ Dat) with, by, at
bei meiner Mutter at my mother's
bei/legen to enclose
das **Beispiel(e)** example
zum Beispiel for example
bekommen to get, receive
belegen to cover
ein **belegtes Brot** open sandwich
Belgien Belgium
die **Bemerkung(en)** die
der **Berg(e)** mountain
beschreiben to describe
beste(r/s) best
am besten the best, best of all
bestellen to order
das **Bett(en)** bed
im Bett in bed
ins Bett gehen to go to bed
der **Bettler(-)** beggar
bezahlen to pay
das **Bier** bier
das **Bild(er)** picture
bilden to build
der **Bildschirm(e)** (TV or computer) screen
die **Bildvokabeln** picture vocabulary
billig cheap
ich **bin** I am (from **sein**)

die **Biologie** biology
bis until
du **bist** you are (from **sein**)
bitte please; don't mention it
wie bitte? pardon? sorry?
bleiben to stay, remain
der **Bleistift(e)** pencil
der **Blitz(e)** lightning
die **Blockflöte(n)** recorder
blöd stupid
die **Bockwurst(¨e)** sausage
die **Bonbons** sweets
die **Bratkartoffeln** fried potatoes
brauchen to need
der **Brief(e)** letter
der **Brieffreund(e)** penfriend (m)
die **Brieffreundin(nen)** penfriend (f)
die **Briefmarke(n)** stamp
die **Brille(n)** glasses
das **Brot(e)** bread
das **Brötchen(-)** roll
der **Bruder(¨)** brother
Brüssel Brussels
das **Buch(¨er)** book
das **Bücherregal(e)** bookshelf
der **Buchstabe(n)** letter of alphabet
der **Buchstabensalat(e)** jumble of letters
bummeln to stroll
der **Bungalow(s)** bungalow
bunt gefärbt brightly painted
die **Butter** butter

C

der **Campingplatz(¨e)** campsite
die **CD (Compact-disc)** CD (compact disc)
chaotisch chaotic
Chemie chemistry
das **chinesische Neujahr** Chinese New Year
die **Chips** (pl) potato crisps
christlich Christian
Christus (Christi) (of) Christ
die **Cola(s)** coca cola
der **Computer(-)** computer
die **Cornflakes** cornflakes
der **Couch(en)** couch
der **Cousin(s)** cousin (m)
die **Cousine(n)** cousin (f)
der **Curryreis** curried rice

D

da there
das **Dach(¨er)** roof
der **Dachboden(¨)** attic
damit with it
Dänemark Denmark
danke thank you
dann then, next
das the (n); that, this; it
das ist this is
daß that

das	**Datum (Daten)** date	
	dauern to last	
	dein(e) your	
	denken an (+ Acc) to think about	
	denn then	
	der/die/das the (m/f/n); he/she/it	
	deshalb therefore	
	deutsch German	
	Deutsch German (lang.)	
	auf Deutsch in German	
	der/die Deutsche German person	
	Deutschland Germany	
	Dezember December	
der	**Dialog(e)** dialogue	
	die the (f/pl); she	
	Dienstag Tuesday	
	dienstags on Tuesdays	
	diese this, these	
	dieselbe, dasselbe, dieselben (pl) the same	
	dir (to) you (Dat)	
die	**Disco(s)** disco	
die	**Diskette(n)** computer disk	
das	**Diskettenlaufwerk(e)** disk drive	
	Diwali Diwali (Hindu festival)	
	doch however, yet, but	
der	**Dokumentarfilm(e)** documentary	
	Donnerstag Thursday	
	donnerstags on Thursdays	
	doof stupid	
das	**Dorf(¨er)** village	
	dort there	
	dran sein to be one's turn	
	jetzt bist du dran now it's your turn	
	drauf on it	
	drei three	
	dreißig thirty	
	dreiunddreißig thirty-three	
	dreizehn thirteen	
	dritte(r/s/n) third	
der	**Drucker(-)** printer	
	du you (informal sing)	
	dumm stupid	
	durch (+ Acc) through	
	durcheinander mixed, muddled up	
die	**Dusche(n)** shower	

E

die	**Ecke(n)** corner	
	in der Ecke in the corner	
	egal equal	
	es ist mir egal it's all the same to me	
das	**Ei(er)** egg	
	ein gekochtes Ei a boiled egg	
	eigen(e) own	
	ein(e) a, an, one	
	ein/füllen to fill in	

das	**Einfamilienhaus(¨er)** detached house	
	einige several, some	
	einmal once; one (portion)	
	einmal Vanille und einmal Schokolade one scoop of vanilla (ice) and one of chocolate	
	eins one	
ein	**Einzelkind** only child	
die	**Einzimmerwohnung(en)** one bedroom flat	
das	**Eis** ice cream	
die	**Eisbude(n)** ice cream stall	
	elf eleven	
die	**Eltern** parents	
am	**Ende (April)** at the end (of April)	
	kommt zu Ende is finishing	
	England England	
der	**Engländer(-)** English man	
die	**Engländerin(nen)** English woman	
	Englisch English (lang.)	
	englisch English	
	Entschuldigung! sorry!	
	er he, it	
die	**Erbse(n)** pea	
die	**Erdbeere(n)** strawberry	
die	**Erde** earth	
	Erdkunde geography	
	ernstlich serious	
	erst only; only just; not until	
	der ist erst 13! he is only just 13!	
	erste(r/s/n) first	
	es it; (sometimes: he/she)	
das	**Essen** food	
	essen to eat	
das	**Eßzimmer(-)** dining-room	
die	**Eßzimmertapete** dining-room wallpaper	
	Europa Europe	

F

das	**Fach(¨er)** subject (at school)	
	fahren to go, travel	
das	**Fahrrad(¨er)** bicycle	
	falsch wrong	
die	**Familie(n)** family	
die	**Familienname(n)** surname, family name	
der	**Fan(s)** fan	
	fangen to catch	
	fantastisch fantastic	
der	**Fastmonat** month of fasting	
	faulenzen to laze around	
	Februar February	
	Federball badminton	
	fehlen to lack, be missing	
der	**Fehler(-)** mistake	
der	**Feiertag(e)** public holiday	
der	**Feierzug(¨e)** procession	
das	**Fenster(-)** window	
die	**Ferien** (pl) holidays	
	machen Sie Ferien? are you going on holiday?	

das	**Ferienhaus(¨er)** holiday home	
die	**Ferienpläne** (pl) holiday plans	
	fern/sehen, fern/gucken to watch television	
das	**Fernsehen** television	
	im Fernsehen on television	
der	**Fernseher** television (set)	
die	**Fernsehsendung(en)** television programme	
	fertig ready	
	fertig/schreiben to complete	
das	**Fest(e)** festival	
das	**Fett(e)** fat	
das	**Feuer(-)** fire	
das	**Feuerwerk(e)** firework	
	finden to find	
er	**fing ... an** he began (from an/fangen)	
der	**Fisch(e)** fish	
	fit fit	
die	**Flasche(n)** bottle	
das	**Fleisch** meat	
	fliegen to fly	
	fließend Wasser running water	
der	**Floh(¨e)** flea	
der	**Flohmarkt(¨e)** flea market	
die	**Flöte(n)** flute	
	folgen to follow	
das	**Foto(s)** photo	
das	**Fotoquiz** photo quiz	
	fragen to ask	
	frag ask	
die	**Frage(n)** question	
die	**Franken(-)** Swiss franc	
	Frankreich France	
	Französisch French (lang.)	
er/sie/es	**fraß** ate (from fressen)	
die	**Frau(en)** woman; Mrs.	
	frei free, vacant, available	
	freistehend freestanding	
	Freitag Friday	
	freitags on Fridays	
die	**Freizeit** free time	
das	**Freizeitwappen** 'leisure shield'	
sich	**freuen auf** (+ Acc) to look forward to	
	ich freue mich auf deinen Besuch I'm looking forward to seeing you	
der	**Freund(e)** friend; boyfriend	
die	**Freundin(nen)** friend; girlfriend	
die	**Frikadelle(n)** rissole	
	frisch fresh	
	frisches Obst fresh fruit	
du	**frißt (from fressen)** you eat, guzzle	
	fröhlich happy	
der	**Frühling** spring (season)	
	im Frühling in spring	
	frühstücken to have breakfast	
	fünf five	
	fünfzehn fifteen	

G

fünfzig fifty
für (+ Acc) for
furchtbar dreadful
fürchterlich awful
Fußball spielen to play football

die **Gabel(n)** fork
ganz quite; whole
gar nicht not at all
die **Garage(n)** garage
der **Garten(˙)** garden
der **Gast(˙e)** guest
geb. (abbr. for **geboren**) born
geben to give
ich gebe mein Geld für CDs aus I spend my money on CDs
Gebirge(-) das mountains
gebraten fried
die **Geburt** birth
der **Geburtstag(e)** birthday
das **Gedeck** place setting
das **Gedicht(e)** poem
gefallen (+ Dat) to like
das gefällt mir I like that
gegrillt grilled
gehen to go, walk
geh go
gehören to belong
was gehört zusammen? what belongs together?
er/sie/es **geht** he/she/it goes
das **geht** it's OK, that's OK
die **Geige(n)** violin
der **Geist(er)** ghost, spirit
der heilige Geist Holy Ghost
böse Geister evil spirits
die **Geisterbahn(en)** ghost train
das **Geld** money
die **Geldsummen** sums of money
die **Gemeinschaft(en)** community
gemischt mixed
das **Gemüse** vegetables
genau! right! exactly!
genug enough
das **Gerede** talk, gossip
die **Gesamtschule(n)** comprehensive school
hat **geschickt** sent
die **Geschichte** history; story
die **Geschwister** brothers and sisters
gest. (abbr. for **gestorben**) died
gesund healthy
gesund essen to eat healthily
das **Getränk(e)** drink
es **gibt** there is, there are (from **geben**)
er/sie/es **ging** he/she/it went (from **gehen**)
die **Gitarre(n)** guitar

das **Glas(˙er)** glass
ein Glas Wein a glass of wine
gleich the same; at once
die **Glotze(n)** goggle-box (television)
der Superglotzer der Woche 'square-eyes' of the week
glücklicherweise luckily
das **Gold** gold, golden
der **Goldfisch(e)** goldfish
der **Gott(˙er)** God, god
der **Grad** temperature, degree
wieviel Grad ist es? what is the temperature?
der **Graf(en)** Count
Graf Dracula Count Dracula
grauenvoll dreadful
Griechenland Greece
der **Groschen(-)** Austrian penny; German 10 Pfennig piece
groß big, large, tall
Großbritannien Great Britain
die **Großmutter(˙)** grandmother
größte biggest, largest, tallest
der **Großvater(˙)** grandfather
das **Grundstück(e)** site, plot of land
die **Gruppe(n)** group
der **Gruß(˙e)** greeting
grüßen to greet
grüß Dich! hallo there!
Guck mal! Look!
gucken to look at, watch
fern/gucken to watch television
das **Gulasch** goulash
die **Gummibärchen** jelly babies/bears
der **Gürtel(-)** belt
gut good, well
gute Nacht! good night!
guten Morgen! good morning, hello
das **Gymnasium (Gymnasien)** grammar school

H

haben to have
das **Hähnchen(-)** chicken
halb half
um halb sieben at half past six
hallo! hello!
das **Halstuch(˙er)** scarf, necktie
halten to stop
der **Hamburger(-)** hamburger
Handball handball
der **Handschuh(e)** glove
du **hast** you have (from **haben**)
er/sie/es **hat** he/she/it has (from **haben**)
ich **hätte gern** I'd like (from **haben**)

die **Hauptschule(n)** secondary school
die **Hauptstadt(˙e)** capital city
die **Hausaufgaben** (pl) homework
das **Haustier(e)** pet
Hauswirtschaft home economics
der **Hbf.** (abbr. of **Hauptbahnhof**) main railway station
das **Heft(e)** exercise book
heiß hot
heißen to be called
wie heißt du? what is your name?
helfen (+ Dat) help
das **Hemd(en)** shirt
der **Herbst** autumn
im Herbst in autumn
der **Herd(e)** cooker, stove
herzlich warm
herzliche Grüße very best wishes
heute today
heute abend this evening
hier here
die **Himbeere(n)** raspberry
hinduistisch Hindu
hinten on the back, behind
hinter (+ Acc/Dat) behind
der **Hit(s)** hit (in music)
die **Hitparade(n)** hit parade, charts
das **Hobby(s)** hobby
das **Hochhaus(˙er)** high-rise building, skyscraper
der **Hochsprung** high jump
hoffentlich hopefully, I hope
der **Honig** honey
hör zu listen (from **zu/hören**)
die **Hose(n)** trousers
das **Hotel(s)** hotel
der **Hund(e)** dog
das **Hündchen(-)** puppy, little dog
hundert hundred
der **Hundertmeterlauf** the 100 metres race
der **Hunger** hunger
der **Hut(˙e)** hat

I

ich I
der **Igel(-)** hedgehog
ihm (to) him/it (Dat)
ihr you; (to) her
ihr(e/n) their; her
im (abbr. of **in dem**) in the
immer always
der **Immobilienmarkt(˙e)** property market
in (+ Acc/Dat) into, in
Informatik information technology
ins (abbr. of **in das**) into the
ins Gebirge to the mountains
insgesamt altogether, in total

interessant interesting
interessiert interested
international international
das **Interview(s)** interview
Irland Ireland
du **ißt** you eat (from **essen**)
er/sie/es **ist** he/she/it is (from **sein**)
Italien Italy

J

ja yes
die **Jacke(n)** jacket
das **Jahr(e)** year
die **Jahreswende** turn of the year
die **Jahreszeit(en)** season
der **Jahrmarkt** funfair
Januar January
die **Jeansjacke(n)** denim jacket
jede(r/s) each, every
jedoch however, yet
jetzt now
  jetzt bist du dran! now it's your turn!
der **Joghurt(s)** yoghurt
jüdisch Jewish
die **Jugendgruppe(n)** youth group
die **Jugendherberge(n)** youth hostel
die/der **Jugendliche/r** young person
Juli July
jung young
der **Junge(n)** boy
Juni June

K

der **Kaffee(s)** coffee
der **Kakao** cocoa, hot chocolate
der **Kalender(-)** calendar
die **Kalorie(n)** calories
  die **Kalorientabelle** calory chart
kalt cold
  kaltes Büffet cold buffet
der **Kamin(e)** chimney, fireplace
der **Kanarienvogel(¨)** canary
das **Kaninchen(-)** rabbit
er/sie/es **kann** he/she/it can (from **können**)
die **Kanne(n)** pot, can
du **kannst** you can (from **können**)
die **Kantine(n)** canteen
das **Kapitel(-)** chapter
kaputt broken, not working
die **Karotte(n)** carrot
die **Karte(n)** map; card
die **Kartoffel(n)** potato
das **Karussell(s)** roundabout
der **Käse** cheese
die **Kassette(n)** cassette
der **Kassettenrecorder(-)** cassette recorder
katastrophal disastrous, catastrophic

das **Kätzchen(-)** kitten
die **Katze(n)** cat
kaufen to buy
kein(e/n) no, none
keinmal not once, never
der **Keks(e)** biscuit
der **Keller(-)** cellar
der **Kellner(-)** waiter
die **Kellnerin(nen)** waitress
die **Kerze(n)** candle
der **Ketchup** ketchup
das **Keyboard(s)** (musical) keyboard
das **Kind(er)** child
die **Kindersendung(en)** children's programme
das **Kino(s)** cinema
klar obvious(ly), clear
  alles klar everything's OK
die **Klarinette(n)** clarinet
die **Klasse(n)** class
klasse! excellent, great
der **Klassenraum(¨e)** classroom
die **klassische Musik** classical music
das **Klavier(e)** piano
die **Kleider** (pl) clothes
der **Kleiderschrank(¨e)** wardrobe
klein small
der **Knoblauch** garlic
kochen to cook
Köln Cologne
komm! come on!
kommen to come
  komm doch heraus! come on out!
  kommst du mit? are you coming with us/me?
die **Komödie(n)** comedy
kompakt compact
die **Konfitüre(n)** jam
können to be able to
kosten to cost
köstlich terrific, great
kreativ creative
der **Kreis(e)** circle
kriegen to get
der **Krimi(s)** thriller, crime series
die **Küche(n)** kitchen
der **Kuchen(-)** cake
die **Kugel(n)** ball, scoop (of ice-cream)
kühl cool, chilly
der **Kühlschrank(¨e)** fridge
der **Kuli(s)** biro, ballpoint pen
die **Kunst** art
die **Kurzschrift** shorthand
der **Kuß (Küsse)** kiss

L

die **Lampe(n)** lamp
das **Land(¨er)** country; countryside
  aufs Land to the country
die **Landkarte(n)** map
lang long
  länger longer

langweilig boring
der **Laptop** laptop computer
Latein latin
der **Lauf(¨e)** race, run
laufen to run, be on
  was läuft? what's on? (cinema, etc)
laut loud
leben to live
der **Leckerbissen** delicacy, titbit
das **Leder** leather
der **Ledergürtel(-)** leather belt
der **Lehrer(-)** teacher (m)
die **Lehrerin(nen)** teacher (f)
die **Leichtathletik** athletics
das **Leichtathletikfest(e)** athletics festival
die **Leinwand** screen
das **Lernziel(e)** learning goal, aim
lesen to read
letzte(r/s) last
  letztes Jahr last year
die **Leute** people
das **Lichtfest** festival of light
die **Liebe** love
  Liebe Anne! dear Anne
  Lieber Paul! dear Paul
lieben to love
der **Liebhaber(-)** sweetheart
Lieblings- favourite
  Lieblingsfach(¨er) favourite subject
am **liebsten** the best, best of all
Liechtenstein Liechtenstein
das **Lied(er)** song
liegen in (+ Dat) to lie, be in
lies read (from **lesen**)
die **Limonade(n)/Limo** lemonade
das **Lineal(e)** ruler
links left, on the left
die **Liste(n)** list
der **Löffel(-)** spoon
los! come on! let's go
  was ist los? what's the matter?
die **Lösung(en)** solution
die **Lücke(n)** gap
  die **Lückensätze** sentences with gaps in
die **Luftmatratze(n)** air mattress
lustig amusing, cheerful
Luxemburg Luxembourg
der **Luxus** luxury
die **Luxuswohnung(en)** luxury flat

M

mach schnell! be quick!
machen to do, make
  machen Sie Ferien? are you going on holiday?
das **Mädchen(-)** girl
die **Mahlzeit(en)** mealtime
  zwischen den Mahlzeiten zu essen to eat between meals

Mai May
das **Make-up** make-up
das **Mal(e)** time
    zum ersten Mal for the first time
    malen to paint
    Mallorca Majorca
    man one, they, people, you
    manchmal sometimes
der **Mann(¨er)** man
die **Margarine** margarine
die **Mark(-), D-Mark** German mark
der **Marktplatz(¨e)** market square, market place
die **Marmelade(n)** jam
    März March
das **Maschinenschreiben** typing
die **Mathematik** mathematics
die **Maus(¨e)** mouse
das **Meer(e)** sea
    am Meer by the sea
    ans Meer to the seaside
die **Meeresfrüchte** (pl) seafood
    mein(e/n/r) my
    in meiner Freizeit in my spare time
    meinen to think
    was meinst du? what do you think?
die **Meinung(en)** opinion
die **meisten** most (people)
    meistens mostly
    melodisch tuneful, melodic
die **Menge(n)** crowd, heap
das **Menü** menu
das **Messer(-)** knife
der **Meter(-)** metre
    mies lousy
    mieten to rent, hire
die **Milch** milk
eine **Million(en)** million
der **Millionär** millionaire
die **Minute(n)** minute
    mit with
das **Mitglied(er)** member
zum **Mitmachen** for joining in
der **Mittag** midday, noon
das **Mittagessen** lunch
    mittelgroß medium-sized
die **Mitternacht** midnight
    Mittwoch Wednesday
    mittwochs on Wednesdays
ich **möchte** I'd like (from **mögen**)
    modern modern
    modernisiert modernised
    mohammedanisch Muslim
der **Mokka(s)** mocha (coffee)
der **Monat(e)** month
    Montag Monday
    am Montag on Monday
der **Morgen(-)** morning
    morgen tomorrow
    morgens in the mornings
    Moskau Moscow
    müde tired

    München Munich
die **Münze(n)** coin
die **Musik** music
das **Musikinstrument(e)** musical instrument
das **Müsli(s)** muesli
ich **muß** I must (from **müssen**)
du **mußt** you must (from **müssen**)
    müssen to have to, must
die **Mutter(¨)** mother
die **Muttersprache(n)** mother tongue

N

    nach (+ Dat) to; after
    nach Holzkirchen to Holzkirchen
    nachmittags in the afternoons
die **Nachrichten** (pl) news
die **Nacht(¨e)** night
    gute Nacht! good night
in der **Nähe von** near
das **Nähen** needlework
der **Name(n)** name
    natürlich! of course!
    neblig foggy
    negativ negative
    nehmen (zu) to take (in)
    nein no
    nett nice
    neu new
    Neujahr New Year
    neun nine
    neunzehn nineteen
    neunzig ninety
    neutral neutral
    nicht not
    nicht mehr no more, no longer
    nicht so gut! not so good!
    nicht wahr? isn't it? aren't you/they? etc
    nicht sehr weit not very far
    nichts nothing
    nichts besonderes nothing special
    nie/niemals never
    niemand no-one
    noch nicht not yet
    nochmal again
    Norddeutschland North Germany
der **Nord** north
    Nordost northeast
    Nordwest northwest
    im Norden in the north
    im Nordwesten in the northwest
    Nordirland Northern Ireland
    normalerweise normally
die **Note(n)** mark, grade
    Notizen machen to make notes
    November November

die **Nudel(n)** noodle, pasta
    null zero
die **Nummer(n)** number
    nur only
die **Nuß (Nüsse)** nut

O

das **Obst** fruit
    oder or
    oft often
    öfter more often
    Oktober October
die **Olive(n)** olive
der **Onkel** uncle
der **Orangensaft** orange juice
das **Orchester(-)** orchestra
der **Ort(e)** place
der **Ost** east
    im Osten in the east
    Ostern Easter
    das Osterei(er) Easter egg
    das Osterfest Eastertime
    der Osterhase(n) Easter bunny
    Österreich Austria
die **Ostsee** Baltic Sea

P

ein **paar Tage** a few days
die **Packung(en)** packet
    eine Packung Chips a packet of crisps
die **Palette(n)** range; artist's palette
der **Papagei(en)** parrot
der **Paprika** green pepper
der **Papst** Pope
der **Park(s)** park
der **Parmesan-Käse** parmesan cheese
der **Partner(-)** partner (m)
die **Partnerin(nen)** partner (f)
    passen zu (+ Dat) to match, go together
die **passende Adresse** the appropriate address
die **Peperoni** (pl) chilli peppers
die **Person(en)** person
der **Pfeffer** pepper
    Pfennig(-) German penny
das **Pferd(e)** horse
    Pfingsten Whitsuntide
das **Pfund(-)** pound
    Physik physics
das **Picknick(s)** picnic
der **Pilz(e)** mushroom
die **Pizzeria(s)** pizzeria
der **Planet(en)** planet
der **Platz(¨e)** place
    Politik politics
die **Polizei** police
die **Pommes frites/Pommes** (pl) chips
die **Portion(en)** portion
    positiv positive

das	**Poster(s)** poster
die	**Postkarte(n)** postcard
	präsentieren present, introduce
der	**Preis(e)** price
die	**Preisliste(n)** price list
	prima! great
	pro per
	pro Woche per week
das	**Programm(e)** programme, computer program
	Prozent per cent
	pünktlich punctual, punctually
die	**Purzelwörter** (pl) jumbled words, anagrams

Q

der	**Quadratmeter(-)** square metre
der	**Quark** soft curd cheese
	Quatsch! rubbish!

R

	rad/fahren, fahren mit dem Rad to go cycling
das	**Radio(s)** radio
	Ramadan Ramadan
der	**Rappen(-)** Swiss centime
	raten to guess
das	**Rätsel(-)** riddle, (crossword) puzzle
die	**Ratte(n)** rat
die	**Ravioli** (pl) ravioli
die	**Realschule(n)** secondary school
	regnen to rain
	rechts right, on the right
	reich rich
die	**Reihenfolge** order
	in der richtigen Reihenfolge in the right order
das	**Reihenhaus("er)** terraced house
der	**Reis** rice
	Reisetips (pl) travel tips
	reiten to ride
die	**Religion** religious studies, religion
die	**Reportage(n)** report
das	**Restaurant(s)** restaurant
das	**Resultat(e)** result
	richtig correct
das	**Riesenrad("er)** big wheel
die	**Rockgruppe(n)** rock group/band
das	**Rollschuhlaufen** roller skating
	Rom Rome
	rot red
	rudern to row
	Rußland Russia

S

der	**Saal(Säle)** room; cinema screen
die	**Saalnummer(n)** room/screen number
die	**Sache(n)** thing
der	**Saft("e)** juice
	sagen to say, tell
	sag mal tell me
er/sie/es	**sah** he/she/it saw (from **sehen**)
die	**Salami(s)** salami
der	**Salat(e)** salat
das	**Salz** salt
	Samstag Saturday
	samstags on Saturdays
der	**Sand** sand
die	**Sandburg(en)** sandcastle
die	**Sardelle(n)** anchovies
der	**Satz("e)** sentence
das	**Saxophon** saxaphone
	Schach spielen to play chess
	schade shame
	wie schade! what a shame!
der	**Schal(s)** scarf
die	**Schale(n)** bowl
das	**Schaschlik(s)** kebab
das	**Schauspiel** play, drama
die	**Scheibe(n)** slice
der	**Schein(e)** banknote
	scheinen to shine
(sich)	**schenken** to give (each other) presents
die	**Schiffschaukel(n)** swing boat
das	**Schild(er)** caption, label, sign
die	**Schildkröte(n)** tortoise
der	**Schilling(-)** Austrian shilling
der	**Schimpanse(n)** chimpanzee
der	**Schinken(-)** ham
	schlafen to sleep
er/sie/es	**schläft** he/she/it sleeps (from **schlafen**)
das	**Schlagzeug** drums
die	**Schlange(n)** snake
	schlecht bad
	schlechte Noten bad marks
der	**Schlüssel(-)** key
	schmecken to taste
	schmeckt das? does that taste good?
	das schmeckt nicht that doesn't taste good
der	**Schnee** snow
	schneien to snow
der	**Schnellimbiß** snack, snack bar
die	**Schokolade(n)** chocolate
der	**Schokoriegel(-)** bar of chocolate
	schon already
	schön fine
	Schottland Scotland
der	**Schrank("e)** cupboard

	Schreib bald! Write soon!
	schreiben to write
	wie schreibt man das? how do you spell that?
der	**Schuh(e)** shoe
die	**Schulaufgaben** (pl) homework
das	**Schulbuch("er)** school book
die	**Schule(n)** school
	die Schule ist aus school is over
der	**Schüler(-)** pupil (boy)
die	**Schülerin(nen)** pupil (girl)
das	**Schülermagazin(e)** school magazine
der	**Schulranzen(-)** satchel
die	**Schuluniform(en)** school uniform
die	**Schüssel(n)** bowl
	schwarz black
der	**Schwarzwald** Black Forest
das	**Schwein(e)** pig, swine
die	**Schweiz** Switzerland
	in der Schweiz in Switzerland
	schwer difficult; heavy
die	**Schwester(n)** sister
	schwimmen to swim
	schwimmen gehen to go swimming
	sechs six
	sechste(n) sixth
	sechzehn sixteen
	sechzig sixty
der	**Seeblick(e)** seaview
das	**Seelachs-filet(s)** sea salmon fillet
das	**Segelboot(e)** sailing boat
	sehr very
ihr	**seid** you are (from **sein**)
	sein to be
	sein(e/r) his, its
	seit since
	seit einer Woche for the past week
die	**Selbstbedienung** self-service
	selten rare, seldom
	September September
die	**Serie(n)** series
der	**Servierlöffel(-)** serving spoon
die	**Serviette(n)** serviette, napkin
das	**Set(s)** place mat
	sie she, it, they; her, them
	sieben seven
	siebte(n) seventh
	siebzehn seventeen
	siebzig seventy
sie	**sind** they are (from **sein**)
das	**sind** that makes; those are
	singen to sing
	ski/fahren, ski/laufen to go ski-ing
der	**Skorpion** Scorpio
	so so, thus
das	**Sofa(s)** sofa
	solange so long as
	solche such

der	**Sommer** summer	
	im Sommer in summer	
	sondern but, rather	
die	**Sonne** sun	
die	**Sonnenbrille(n)** sun glasses	
die	**Sonnencreme** sun cream	
der	**Sonnenschirm(e)** sun shade	
	Sonntag Sunday	
	sonntags on Sundays	
	sortieren to sort out	
die	**Soße(n)** sauce, gravy	
	Sozialkunde social studies	
	Spanien Spain	
	sparen to save	
	spät late	
	wie spät ist es? what time is it?	
	spazieren/gehen to go for a walk	
der	**Speerwurf** throwing the javelin	
die	**Speisekarte(n)** menu	
das	**Spiegelbild(er)** reflection	
das	**Spiegelei(er)** fried egg	
das	**Spiel(e)** game	
	spielen to play	
die	**Spielshow(s)** gameshow	
die	**Spinne(n)** spider	
	Sport PE, sport	
die	**Sporthelden** (pl) sporting heroes	
der	**Sportklub(s)** sports club	
die	**Sprechblase(n)** speech bubble	
er/sie/es	**spricht** he/she/it speaks (from **sprechen**)	
	Squash squash	
die	**Stabheuschrecke(n)** stick insect	
die	**Stadtmitte(n)** city centre	
am	**Stadtrand** on the edge of town	
der	**Stammbaum(¨e)** family tree	
	stehen to stand	
der	**Sticker(e)** badge	
der	**Stiefbruder(¨)** stepbrother	
der	**Stiefel(-)** boot	
die	**Stiefmutter(¨)** stepmother	
die	**Stiefschwester(n)** stepsister	
der	**Stiefvater(¨)** stepfather	
	still quiet(ly)	
	stimmen to be right	
	stimmt das? is that OK?	
	stinken to smell, stink	
	stinklangweilig deadly boring	
der	**Strand(¨e)** beach	
der	**Strandkorb(¨e)** wicker beach chair	
die	**Straße(n)** street, road	
	auf der Straße on the street	
die	**Straßenkinder** (pl) street children	
das	**Straßentheaterstück(e)** street theatre play	
der	**Streit(e)** quarrel	
	streiten to argue	

	streng strict	
	stubenrein house-trained	
das	**Stück(e)** piece	
ein	**Stückchen Brot** a piece of bread	
die	**Studentenwohnung(en)** student flat	
die	**Studiodiskussion(en)** studio discussion	
der	**Stuhl(¨e)** chair	
die	**Stunde(n)** hour	
der	**Stundenplan(¨e)** school timetable	
	suchen to look for	
	Süd south	
	im Süden in the south	
	im Südosten in the southeast	
	im Südwesten in the southwest	
	Süddeutschland South Germany	
die	**Summe(n)** sum, total	
die	**Suppe(n)** soup	
das	**Surfbrett(er)** surfboard	
	surfen to go surfing	
die	**Süßigkeit(en)** sweet	
	Sylvester New Year's Eve	
das	**Symbol(e)** symbol	
die	**Symphonie(n)** symphony	

T

die	**Tabelle(n)** table, chart	
die	**Tafel(n)** board; bar (of chocolate)	
der	**Tag(e)** day	
	eines Tages one day	
	guten Tag! hello, good day	
der	**Tageslichtprojektor(en)** overhead projector	
die	**Tagesroutine** daily routine	
die	**Tagesschau** the News	
das	**Tal(¨er)** valley	
die	**Talkshow(s)** talkshow	
die	**Tante(n)** aunt	
	tanzen to dance	
die	**Tapete(n)** wallpaper	
die	**Tastatur** keyboard	
	tausend thousand	
der	**Tee** tea	
der	**Teelöffel(-)** teaspoon	
der	**Teenager(s)** teenager	
die	**Telefonnummer(n)** telephone number	
die	**Telefonzelle(n)** phone box	
der	**Teller(-)** plate	
die	**Temperatur(en)** temperature	
	Tennis tennis	
der	**Tennisschläger(-)** tennis racquet	
die	**Terrasse(n)** terrace	
das	**Thema(Themen)** theme, subject	
das	**Tier(e)** animal	
der	**Tip(s)** tip	
	tippen to type	

der	**Tippfehler(-)** typing mistake	
der	**Tisch(e)** table	
die	**Tischdecke(n)** table cloth	
der	**Titel(-)** title, caption	
der	**Toast(s)** (slice of) toast	
die	**Toilette(n)** toilet	
	toll great, terrific	
die	**Tomate(n)** tomato	
die	**Tomatensuppe** tomato soup	
	total completely, totally	
	total modernisiert fully modernised	
der	**Tourist(en)** tourist	
das	**Trampolin(e)** trampoline	
das	**Traumhaus(¨er)** dream house	
der	**Treffpunkt** meeting place	
	treiben to do (sport)	
die	**Treppe(n)** staircase, stairs	
der	**Trickfilm(e)** animated cartoon	
	trinken to drink	
die	**Trompete(n)** trumpet	
	tschüß! bye!	
das	**T-Shirt** T-shirt	
das	**Tuch(¨er)** towel, cloth	
	tun to do	
	es tut mir leid I'm sorry	
der	**Tunnel(s)** tunnel	
die	**Tür(en)** door	
die	**Turnschuhe** (pl) trainers (shoes)	
	typisch typical	

U

	üben to practise	
	über over, on	
	überall everywhere	
	überhaupt at all	
	überhaupt nicht not at all	
	übernachten to spend the night	
die	**Uhr(en)** hour; time; clock	
	wieviel Uhr ist es? what time is it?	
die	**Uhrzeit** time of day	
	um at, around	
	um halb sieben at half past six	
	um … zu in order to	
	um/bringen to kill	
	ich bringe ihn um! I'll kill him!	
die	**Umfrage(n)** survey	
der	**Umschlag(¨e)** envelope	
	um/wechseln to change (money)	
	und and	
	ungefähr approximately, about	
	ungesund unhealthy, unhealthily	
	ungewöhnlich unusual	
	unglaublich unbelievable, incredible	
	unglücklich unhappy	
die	**Unterkunft** accommodation	
der	**Unterricht** teaching, lessons	

die **Untertasse(n)** saucer
ununterbrochen uninterrupted
der **Urlaub(e)** holiday
   im Urlaub on holiday
die **USA** USA

V

der **Valentinstag** Valentine's Day
die **Vanille** vanilla (ice cream)
der **Vater(¨)** father
verbringen to spend (time)
Verdammt! Damn! Blast!
vergessen to forget
verkaufen to sell
   zu verkaufen for sale
das **Verkaufsbüro(s)** sales office
verlassen to leave
die **Versammlung** assembly
verschieden various
vervollständigen to complete
viel besser much better
vier four
das **Viertel(-)** quarter
   es ist Viertel nach zwei it's quarter past two
vierte(n) fourth
vierzehn fourteen
vierzig forty
Volleyball volleyball
von from; by
vor/lesen read aloud
vor/stellen present, introduce
vorn on the front, at the front
der **Vorname(n)** first name
Vorsicht! Be careful!

W

wählen to choose
der **Wald(¨er)** wood
Wales Wales
der **Walkman** Walkman
wann? when?
er/sie/es **war** he/she/it was (from **sein**)
das **wäre** it would be, that would be (from **sein**)
Warschau Warsaw
warten auf (+ Acc) to wait for
was? what?
was für ...? what kind of ...?
sich **waschen** to have a wash, wash oneself
die **Waschmaschine(n)** washing machine
das **Wasser** water
wechseln to exchange
weh/tun to hurt, harm
Weihnachten Christmas
   Weihnachtsgeschenke (pl) Christmas presents
   Weihnachtslieder (pl) Christmas carols
weiß white
der **Weitsprung** long jump
welche(r/s) which

der **Wellensittich(e)** budgerigar
die **Welt** world
   auf der Welt in the world
die **Weltkarte** map of the world
wenig little
weniger (als) less (than)
wer? who?
die **Werbung(en)** advert, advertising
werken to work
West west
   im (Wilden) Westen in the (wild) west
   im Südwesten in the southwest
die **Weste(n)** waistcoat
das **Wetter** weather
wie? how?
   wie geht's? how are things?
   wie heißt dein Onkel? what's your uncle called?
   wie ist das Wetter? what is the weather like?
   wie ist dein Haus? what is your house like?
   wie schade! what a shame
   wie bitte? pardon? sorry?
   wie lange? how long?
   wieviel? wie viele? how much? how many?
wieder again
wieder/finden to find again
wiederholen repeat
Wien Vienna
wieso? for what reason?
windig windy
der **Winter** winter
   im Winter in winter
wir we
wissen to know
die **Wissenschaft** science
wo? where?
die **Woche(n)** week
wofür? for what (reason)?
   wofür sparst du dein Geld? what are you saving up for?
woher? from where?
   woher kommst du? where are you from?
wohin? where to?
   wo fährst du hin? where are you going?
wohnen to live
der **Wohnort(e)** place, town of residence
der **Wohnwagen(-)** caravan
wollen to want to, wish to
das **Wort(¨er)** word
das **Wörterbuch(¨er)** dictionary
wozu? to what?
   was paßt wozu? what matches what?
wunderbar wonderful
der **Wunsch(¨e)** wish
   auf Wunsch on request

die **Wurst(¨e)** sausage
die **Wüste(n)** desert
die **Wüstenmaus(¨e)** gerbil

Z

die **Zahl(en)** number, figure
zahlen to count
das **Zahlenrätsel(-)** number puzzle
zahlreich numerous, many
zehn ten
zeichnen to draw
zeigen auf (+Acc) to show, point to
die **Zeitschrift(en)** magazine
die **Zeitung(en)** newspaper
das **Zelt(e)** tent
die **Ziege(n)** goat
ziemlich rather, quite
das **Zimmer(-)** room
die **Zitrone(n)** lemon
zu too; at; to
   zu alt too old
   zu Hause at home
   zu Gast sein to be someone's guest
zu/hören to listen
der **Zucker** sugar
zünden to light
der **Zungenbrecher(-)** tongue-twister
zurück back
zusammen together
die **Zutaten** (pl) ingredients
zuviel too much
zwanzig twenty
zwei two
zweimal twice
   zweimal Pommes frites two portions of chips
zweite(n) second
die **Zwiebel(n)** onion
zwischen between
zwölf twelve

A

a, an, one ein(e)
to be able to können
abroad das Ausland
accommodation die Unterkunft
activity die Aktivität(en)
address die Adresse(n)
adventure das Abenteuer(-)
advert, advertising die Werbung(en)
after nach (+ Dat)
afternoon der Nachmittag
 in the afternoons nachmittags
again wieder, nochmal
air mattress die Luftmatratze(n)
alphabet puzzle das Alphabeträtsel(-)
all alle
 all the best! alles Gute!
 all together insgesamt
alone allein
alphabet das Alphabet
alphabet song das Alphabetlied(er)
the Alps die Alpen
already schon
also, too auch
always immer
I am ich bin (from sein)
America Amerika
American amerikanisch
amusing, cheerful lustig
anagrams Purzelwörter (pl)
anchovies die Sardelle(n)
and und
animal das Tier(e)
animated cartoon der Trickfilm(e)
anonymously anonym
answer die Antwort(-en)
to answer beantworten
apple der Apfel(¨)
apple juice der Apfelsaft
approximately, about ungefähr
April April
you are du bist, ihr seid, Sie sind (from sein)
 they are sie sind (from sein)
 we are wir sind (from sein)
 aren't you? aren't they? isn't it? etc nicht wahr?
to argue streiten
art Kunst
to ask fragen
assembly die Versammlung
assembly hall die Aula (Aulen)
at um, bei
 at my mother's bei meiner Mutter
 at half past six um halb sieben
 at all gar, überhaupt
he ate aß (from essen), fraß (from fressen)
Athens Athen
athlete der Athlet(en)
athletics die Leichathletik
athletics festival das Leichtathletikfest(e)
attic der Dachboden(¨)
August August
aunt die Tante(n)
Australia Australien
Austria Österreich
Austrian shilling der Schilling(-)
Austrian penny der Groschen(-)
autumn der Herbst
 in autumn im Herbst
awful fürchterlich

B

baby das Baby(s)
baby photo das Babyfoto(s)
back zurück
bad schlecht
 bad marks schlechte Noten
badge der Sticker(e)
badminton Federball
to bake backen
baker's die Bäckerei(en)
balcony der Balkon(s)
ballpoint pen der Kuli(s)
Baltic Sea die Ostsee
banana die Banane(n)
banknote der Schein(e)
bar of chocolate der Schokoriegel(-), die Tafel(n) Schokolade
basketball Basketball
bath, bathing das Bad(¨er)
bath towel das Badetuch(¨er)
bath(tub) die Badewanne(n)
bathroom Badezimmer(-)
beach der Strand(¨e)
 beach chair (wicker) der Strandkorb(¨e)
bed das Bett(en)
 in bed im Bett
 to go to bed ins Bett gehen
beer das Bier
beggar der Bettler(-)
he began er fing an (from an/fangen)
to begin beginnen, an/fangen
beginning der Anfang(¨e), der Beginn
 at the beginning of April am Anfang April
behind hinten; hinter (+Acc/Dat)
Belgium Belgien

C

to belong gehören
belt der Gürtel(-)
best beste(r/s)
 the best, best of all am besten, am liebsten
between zwischen, zwischendurch
bicycle das Fahrrad(¨er), das Rad(¨er)
big groß
 biggest größte
 big dipper die Achterbahn(en)
 big wheel das Riesenrad(¨er)
biology Biologie
birth die Geburt
birthday der Geburtstag(e)
biscuit der Keks(e)
black schwarz
Black Forest Schwarzwald
board die Tafel(n)
boiled egg ein gekochtes Ei
book das Buch(¨er)
bookshelf das Bücherregal(e)
boot der Stiefel(-)
boring langweilig
bottle die Flasche(n)
bowl die Schale(n), die Schüssel(n)
boy der Junge(n)
bread das Brot(e)
bright hell
brightly coloured bunt gefärbt
broken, not working kaputt
brother der Bruder(¨)
brothers and sisters die Geschwister
Brussels Brüssel
budgerigar der Wellensittich(e)
bungalow der Bungalow(s)
but aber; sondern; doch
butter die Butter
to buy kaufen
by the sea am Meer, an der See
bye! tschüs! tschüß!

cake der Kuchen(-)
calendar der Kalender(-)
to be called heißen
 what is your name? wie heißt du?
calories die Kalorien (pl)
campsite der Campingplatz(¨e)
he/she/it can er/sie/es kann
you can du kannst (from können)
canary der Kanarienvogel(¨)
candle die Kerze(n)
canteen die Kantine(n)
capital city die Hauptstadt(¨e)
caption, sign das Schild(er)

car das Auto
  20 minutes by car from Hamburg 20 Autominuten von Hamburg
caravan der Wohnwagen(-)
card die Karte(n)
be **careful!** Vorsicht!
carrot die Karotte(n)
cassette die Kassette(n)
cassette recorder der Kassettenrecorder(-)
cat die Katze(n)
catch fangen
CD die CD
cellar der Keller(-)
chair der Stuhl("e)
to **change (money)** wechseln, umwechseln
chaotic chaotisch
chapter das Kapitel(-)
cheap billig
cheese der Käse
chemistry Chemie
chess Schach
chicken das Hähnchen(-)
child das Kind(er)
children's (television) programme die Kindersendung(en)
chillis die Peperoni (pl)
chimney der Kamin(e)
chimpanzee der Schimpanse(n)
Chinese New Year das chinesische Neujahr
chips Pommes frites, Pommes
chocolate die Schokolade(n)
  hot chocolate der Kakao
to **choose** wählen
Christ Christus (**of Christ** Christi)
Christian christlich
Christmas Weihnachten
  Christmas carol das Weihnachtslied(er)
  Christmas present das Weihnachtsgeschenk(e)
cinema das Kino(s)
  cinema screen der Saal
  cinema screen number die Saalnummer(n)
circle der Kreis(e)
city centre die Stadtmitte(n)
clarinet die Klarinette(n)
class die Klasse(n)
classical music klassische Musik
classroom der Klassenraum("e)
clock die Uhr(en)
clothes die Kleider (pl)
coca cola die Cola(s)
coffee der Kaffee(s)
coin die Münze(n)
cold kalt

cold buffet das kaltes Büffet
Cologne Köln
to **come** kommen
  come on out! komm doch heraus!
  come on! komm! los!
comedy die Komödie
community die Gemeinschaft(en)
compact kompakt
to **complete** vervollständigen
comprehensive school die Gesamtschule(n)
computer der Computer(-)
  computer disk die Diskette(n)
  computer fan der Computerfan(s)
to **cook** kochen, backen
cooker, stove der Herd(e)
cool, chilly kühl
corner die Ecke(n)
  in the corner in der Ecke
cornflakes die Cornflakes
correct richtig
to **cost** kosten
couch der Couch(en)
Count der Graf(en)
  Count Dracula Graf Dracula
to **count** zahlen
country, countryside das Land("er)
  to the country aufs Land
of **course!** natürlich!
cousin der Cousin(s), die Cousine(n)
creative kreativ
crowd die Menge(n)
cupboard der Schrank("e)
to go **cycling** mit dem Rad fahren, rad/fahren

daily routine die Tagesroutine
Damn! Verdammt!
to **dance** tanzen
date das Datum (Daten)
day der Tag(e)
Dear (+ name) Liebe (Anne)! Lieber (Paul)!
December Dezember
delicacy, titbit der Leckerbissen
denim jacket die Jeansjacke(n)
Denmark Dänemark
to **describe** beschreiben
desert die Wüste(n)
detached house das Einfamilienhaus("er)
dialogue der Dialog(e)
dictionary das Wörterbuch("er)

different (from) anders (als)
difficult schwer
dining-room das Eßzimmer(-)
disastrous, catastrophic katastrophal
disco die Disco(s)
disk die Diskette(n)
disk drive das Diskettenlaufwerk(e)
display, notice die Anzeige(n)
Diwali Diwali
to **do, make** machen
to **do (sport)** treiben
documentary der Dokumentarfilm(e)
dodgems der Autoscooter(-)
dog der Hund(e)
door die Tür(en)
to **draw** zeichnen
dreadful furchtbar, grauenvoll
dream house das Traumhaus("er)
drink das Getränk(e)
to **drink** trinken
to **drive away (evil spirits)** (böse Geister) aus/treiben
drums das Schlagzeug

each, every jede(r/s)
earth die Erde
east Ost
  in the east im Osten
Easter Ostern
  Easter bunny der Osterhase(n)
  Easter egg das Osterei(er)
to **eat** essen
  you eat du ißt
  you eat, guzzle du frißt (**from** fressen)
to **eat between meals** zwischen den Mahlzeiten essen
on the **edge of town** am Stadtrand
egg das Ei(er)
eight acht
eighteen achtzehn
eighty achtzig
eleven elf
enclose bei/legen
end das Ende
  at the end of April am Ende April
England England
  English englisch
  English (lang.) Englisch
  English person der Engländer(-), die Engländerin(nen)
enough genug
envelope der Umschlag("e)
equal egal
  it's all the same to me es ist mir egal
Europe Europa

evening der Abend(e)
  in the evenings abends
  evening meal das Abendessen, das Abendbrot
every jede(r/s)
everywhere überall
evil spirits böse Geister
exactly! genau!
example das Beispiel(e)
  for example zum Beispiel
excellent, great Klasse!
to **exchange** wechseln, umwechseln
excuse die Ausrede(n)
exercise book das Heft(e)

F

family die Familie(n)
  family tree der Stammbaum
fantastic fantastisch
far weit
fat das Fett(e)
father der Vater(¨)
favourite Lieblings-
  favourite subjects Lieblingsfächer
February Februar
festival das Fest(e)
  festival of light das Lichtfest, Diwali
a **few days** ein paar Tage
fifteen fünfzehn
fifty fünfzig
figure (num.) die Zahl(en)
to **fill in** ein/füllen
to **find** finden
fine schön
is **finishing** kommt zu Ende
fire das Feuer(-)
fireplace der Kamin(e)
firework das Feuerwerk(e)
first erste(r/s)
first name der Vorname(n)
fish der Fisch(e)
to **fit, suit** an/passen
fit fit
five fünf
flea der Floh(¨e)
  flea market Flohmarkt(¨e)
flute die Flöte(n)
to **fly** fliegen
foggy neblig
to **follow** folgen
food das Essen
to play **football** Fußball spielen
for für (+ Acc)
  to go for a walk spazieren/gehen
  for example zum Beispiel
  for sale zu verkaufen
  for what reason? wieso?
to **forget** vergessen
  I've forgotten ich hab's vergessen

fork die Gabel(n)
forty vierzig
four vier
fourteen vierzehn
fourth vierte(n)
France Frankreich
free, vacant, available frei
free time die Freizeit
freestanding freistehend
Friday Freitag
  on Fridays freitags
French französisch
French (lang.) Französisch
fresh frisch
  fresh fruit frisches Obst
fridge der Kühlschrank(¨e)
fried gebraten
  fried egg das Spiegelei(er)
  fried potatoes die Bratkartoffeln (pl)
  fried sausage die Bratwurst(¨e)
friend (f), girlfriend die Freundin
friend (m), boyfriend der Freund
from aus, von
in **front, at the front** vorn
fruit das Obst
fully modernised total modernisiert
funfair der Jahrmarkt

G

game das Spiel(e)
gameshow die Spielshow
gap die Lücke(n)
garage die Garage(n)
garden der Garten(¨)
garlic der Knoblauch
geography Erdkunde
gerbil die Wüstenmaus(¨e)
Germany Deutschland
  German deutsch
  German (lang.) Deutsch
  in German auf Deutsch
  German mark die Mark(-), D-Mark
  German penny der Pfennig(-)
  German person der/die Deutsche
to **get** kriegen, bekommen
to **get up** auf/stehen
  get up! Steh auf!
ghost der Geist(er)
  ghost train die Geisterbahn(en)
girl das Mädchen(-)
to **give** geben, schenken
at a **glance** auf einen Blick
glass das Glas(¨er)
  a glass of coke ein Glas Cola
glasses die Brille(n)
glove der Handschuh(e)

to **go, walk** gehen
  to go, travel fahren
  to go out aus/gehen
goat die Ziege(n)
God, god der Gott(¨er)
gold, golden das Gold
goldfish der Goldfisch(e)
good, well gut
  a good excuse eine gute Ausrede
  Good morning! Hello! guten Morgen!
  Good night! Gute Nacht!
goulash das Gulasch
grammar school das Gymnasium(Gymnasien)
grandfather der Großvater(¨)
grandmother die Großmutter(¨)
gravy die Soße(n)
great, terrific toll! prima!
Great Britain Großbritannien
Greece Griechenland
to **greet** grüßen
greeting der Gruß(¨e)
grilled gegrillt
group die Gruppe(n)
to **guess** raten
guest der Gast(¨e)
  to be someone's guest zu Gast sein
guitar die Gitarre(n)

H

half halb
  at half past six um halb sieben
  one and a half anderthalb
ham der Schinken(-)
hamburger der Hamburger(-)
handball Handball
happy fröhlich
hat der Hut(¨e)
to **have** haben
to **have to, must** müssen
to **have breakfast** frühstücken
he er
healthy gesund
  healthy eating gesund essen
hedgehog der Igel(-)
Hello! Hallo!
to **help** helfen (+ Dat)
her sie; ihr; ihr(e)
here hier
heroes of sport Sporthelden
high jump der Hochsprung
high-rise building, skyscraper das Hochhaus(¨er)
him ihn; ihm
Hindu hinduistisch
to **hire, rent** mieten
his sein(e)
history Geschichte
hit (in music) der Hit(s)

hit parade, charts die Hitparade(n)
hobby das Hobby(s)
holiday der Urlaub(e)
  holidays die Ferien (pl)
  holiday home das Ferienhaus(¨er)
  holiday plans die Ferienpläne (pl)
Holland Holland
home economics Hauswirtschaft
homework die Hausaufgaben, Schulaufgaben (pl)
honey der Honig
hopefully, I hope hoffentlich
horse das Pferd(e)
hot heiß
  hot chocolate der Kakao
hotel das Hotel(s)
hour die Stunde(n), die Uhr
  what time is it? wieviel Uhr ist es?
house das Haus(¨er)
  detached house das Einfamilienhaus(¨er)
  semi-detached house das Doppelhaus(¨er)
  terraced house das Reihenhaus(¨er)
  house-trained stubenrein
how? wie?
  how are things? wie geht's?
  how do you spell that? wie schreibt man das?
  how old are you? wie alt bist du?
how long? wie lange?
how much? how many? wieviel? wie viele?
however doch, jedoch
hundred hundert
hunger der Hunger
to **hurt, harm** weh/tun

I

I ich
ice cream das Eis
ice cream stall die Eisbude(n)
in in (+ Dat)
  in the im **(abbr. of** in dem**)**, ins **(abbr. of** in das**)**
information technology Informatik
ingredients die Zutaten (pl)
instrument das Instrument(e)
interesting interessant
interested interessiert
international international
interview das Interview(s)
into in (+ Acc)
  into the ins **(abbr. of** in das**)**
Ireland Irland

he/she/it is er/sie/es ist **(from** sein**)**
  there is/are es gibt **(from** geben**)**
it es; er, sie
Italy Italien

J

jacket die Jacke(n)
jam die Konfitüre(n), die Marmelade(n)
January Januar
jelly babies die Gummibärchen (pl)
Jewish jüdisch
for **joining in** zum Mitmachen
juice der Saft(¨e)
July Juli
June Juni
just erst
  he is only just 13! der ist erst 13!

K

kebab das Schaschlik(s)
ketchup der Ketchup
key der Schlüssel(-)
keyboard (music) das Keyboard, **(computer)** die Tastatur
to **kill, murder** um/bringen
  I'll murder him! ich bringe ihn um!
kiss der Kuß (Küsse)
kitchen die Küche(n)
kitten das Kätzchen(-)
knife das Messer(-)
to **know** wissen

L

lamp die Lampe(n)
laptop computer der Laptop
large groß
last letzte(r/s)
to **last** dauern
late spät
Latin Latein
to **laze around** faulenzen
leather das Leder
  leather belt der Ledergürtel(-)
to **leave** verlassen
(on the) **left** links
lemon die Zitrone(n)
lemonade die Limonade(n), Limo
less (than) weniger (als)
lesson die Stunde(n); **(subject)** das Fach(¨er)
  lessons begin at 8.00 der Unterricht beginnt um acht Uhr
letter der Brief(e)
  letter (of alphabet) der Buchstabe(n)

Liechtenstein Liechtenstein
to **light** zünden
lightning der Blitz(e)
to **like** gefallen (+ Dat)
  I like that das gefällt mir
  I'd like ich hätte gern, ich möchte
list die Liste(n)
to **listen** zu/hören
  listen hör zu
little klein; wenig
to **live** wohnen, leben
long lang
  longer länger
  long jump der Weitsprung
to **look at, watch** gucken, an/sehen
  to look for suchen
  to look forward to sich freuen auf (+ Acc)
  Look! Guck mal!
loud laut
lousy mies
to **love** lieben
  love die Liebe
luckily glücklicherweise
lunch das Mittagessen
Luxembourg Luxemburg
luxury der Luxus
  luxury flat die Luxuswohnung

M

magazine die Zeitschrift(en), das Magazin(e)
Majorca Mallorca
make-up das Make-up
man der Mann(¨er)
map die Karte(n), die Landkarte(n)
map of the world die Weltkarte(n)
March März
margarine die Margarine
mark, grade die Note(n)
market place der Marktplatz(¨e)
to **match** passen zu (+ Dat)
mathematics die Mathematik, Mathe
what's the matter? was ist los?
May Mai
meat das Fleisch
medium-sized mittelgroß
meeting place der Treffpunkt
member das Mitglied(er)
menu das Menü(s); die Speisekarte(n)
metre der Meter(-)
  square metre der Quadratmeter(-)
midday Mittag
midnight Mitternacht
milk die Milch
million eine Million(en)
millionaire der Millionär

minute die Minute(n)
to be **missing** fehlen
mistake der Fehler(-)
mixed, muddled up durcheinander, gemischt
mocha (coffee) der Mokka
modern modern
modernised modernisiert
Mohammedan Muslim
Monday Montag
on Monday am Montag
money das Geld
month der Monat(e)
more often öfter
morning der Morgen(-)
in the mornings morgens
Moscow Moskau
most people die meisten
mostly meistens
mother die Mutter(")
mother tongue die Muttersprache(n)
mountain der Berg(e)
mountains das Gebirge(-)
to the mountains ins Gebirge
mouse die Maus("e)
much better viel besser
muesli das Müsli(s)
Munich München
mushroom der Pilz(e)
music die Musik
you **must (from** müssen**)** du mußt
my mein(e)

N

name der Name(n)
what is your name? wie heißt du?
near in der Nähe von
to **need** brauchen
needlework Nähen
negative negativ
neutral neutral
never nie, niemals
new neu
New Year Neujahr
New Year's Eve Sylvester
the **News** die Tagesschau, die Nachrichten (pl)
newspaper die Zeitung(en)
nice nett
night die Nacht("e)
nine neun
nineteen neunzehn
ninety neunzig
no, none kein(e)
no nein
no more, no longer nicht mehr
noodle, pasta die Nudel(n)
no-one niemand
normally normalerweise
north Nord
in the north im Norden
northeast Nordost

north Germany Norddeutschland
Northern Ireland Nordirland
not nicht
not at all gar nicht, überhaupt nicht
not far nicht weit
not so good! nicht so gut!
not yet noch nicht
to make **notes** Notizen machen
nothing special nichts besonderes
November November
now jetzt
number die Nummer(n), die Zahl(en)
number puzzle das Zahlenrätsel
numerous zahlreich
nut die Nuß(Nüsse)

O

observation die Bemerkung(en)
obvious(ly) klar
October Oktober
often oft
more often öfter
is that **OK** stimmt das?
it's OK das geht
old alt
I'm 13 years old ich bin 13 Jahre alt
old man der Alte(n)
olive die Olive(n)
on auf
on it drauf
on Monday am Montag
on Tuesdays dienstags
once einmal
one eins; ein(e); einmal
one, they, people, you man
one and a half anderthalb
one bedroom flat die Einzimmerwohnung(en)
one day eines Tages
onion die Zwiebel(n)
only nur; erst
only child ein Einzelkind
open sandwich belegtes Brot
opinion die Meinung(en)
or oder
orange juice der Orangensaft
orchestra das Orchester(-)
to **order** bestellen
order die Reihenfolge
in the right order in der richtigen Reihenfolge
other andere(r/s)
out aus
over über
overhead projector der Tageslichtprojektor
own eigen(e)

P

packet of crisps eine Packung Chips
paint malen
palette (artist's) die Palette
pardon? wie bitte?
parents die Eltern
park der Park(s)
parmesan cheese der Parmesan-Käse
parrot der Papagei(en)
partner die Partnerin(nen), der Partner(-)
to **pay** bezahlen
PE, sport Sport
pea die Erbse(n)
pencil der Bleistift(e)
penfriend der Brieffreund(e), die Brieffreundin(nen)
people die Leute (pl)
pepper der Pfeffer
green pepper der Paprika
percent Prozent
person die Person(en)
per week pro Woche
pet das Haustier(e)
phone box die Telefonzelle(n)
photo das Foto(s)
photo quiz das Fotoquiz
physics Physik
piano das Klavier(e)
picnic das Picknick(s)
picture das Bild(er)
piece das Stück(e)
a **piece of bread** ein Stückchen Brot
pig das Schwein(e)
pizzeria die Pizzeria(s)
place der Ort(e)
(seat) der Platz("e)
(town of residence) der Wohnort(e)
place mat das Set(s)
place setting das Gedeck(e)
planet der Planet(en)
plate der Teller(-)
play, drama das Schauspiel(e)
to **play** spielen
please bitte
poem das Gedicht(e)
to **point to** zeigen auf (+ Acc)
police die Polizei
politics Politik
poor arm
portion die Portion(en)
positive positiv
postcard die Postkarte(n)
poster das Poster(s)
pot, can die Kanne(n)
potato die Kartoffel(n)
potato crisps die Chips (pl)
pound das Pfund
to **practise** üben

present das Geschenk(e)
to **present, introduce**
präsentieren, vor/stellen
price der Preis(e)
price list die Preisliste(n)
printer der Drucker(-)
procession der Feierzug("e)
programme das Programm(e)
property market der
Immobilienmarkt("e)
public holiday der
Feiertag(e)
punctual, punctually
pünktlich
pupil der Schüler(-), die
Schülerin(nen)
puppy das Hündchen(-)
puzzle das Rätsel(-)

Q

quarrel der Streit(e)
quarter das Viertel
it's quarter past two es ist
Viertel nach zwei
question die Frage(n)
quick(ly) schnell
be quick! mach schnell!
quiet(ly) still
quite ganz

R

rabbit das Kaninchen(-)
race, run der Lauf("e)
radio das Radio(s)
on the radio im Radio
to **rain** regnen
Ramadan Ramadan
rarely, seldom selten
raspberry die Himbeere(n)
rat die Ratte(n)
rather, quite ziemlich
ravioli die Ravioli
to **read** lesen
to **read aloud** vor/lesen
ready fertig
recorder die Blockflöte(n)
red rot
reflection das Spiegelbild
religious studies, religion
Religion
to **rent, hire** mieten
to **repeat** wiederholen
report die Reportage(n)
on **request** auf Wunsch
restaurant das Restaurant(s)
result das Resultat(e)
resurrection die
Auferstehung
rice der Reis
rich reich
riddle, puzzle das Rätsel(-)
to **ride** reiten
right, correct richtig
right! exactly! genau!
(on the) right rechts

is that right? stimmt das?
rissole die Frikadelle(n)
rock group/band die
Rockgruppe(n)
roll das Brötchen(-)
roller skating das
Rollschuhlaufen
Rome Rom
roof das Dach("er)
room der Saal(Säle)
roundabout das Karussell(s)
to **row** rudern
rubbish! Quatsch!
ruler das Lineal(e)
to **run, be on** laufen
running water fließend
Wasser
Russia Rußland

S

sailing boat das Segelboot(e)
salami die Salami(s)
salat der Salat (-)
sales office das
Verkaufsbüro(s)
salt das Salz
the **same** dieselbe/dasselbe/
diesselben; gleich
sand der Sand
sandcastle die Sandburg(en)
satchel der Schulranzen(-)
Saturday Samstag
on Saturdays samstags
sauce, gravy die Soße(n)
saucer die Untertasse(n)
sausage die Wurst("e),
Bockwurst, Bratwurst
to **save** sparen
I/he/she **saw** sah (from **sehen**)
saxaphone das Saxophon
to **say, tell** sagen
scarf der Schal(s), das
Halstuch("er)
school die Schule(n)
in/at school in der Schule
school is over die Schule
ist aus
school book das
Schulbuch("er)
school hall die Aula(Aulen)
school magazine das
Schülermagazin(e)
school timetable der
Stundenplan("e)
school uniform die
Schuluniform(en)
science Wissenschaft
scoop (of ice-cream) die
Kugel(n)
Scorpio der Skorpion
Scotland Schottland
screen (TV or computer) der
Bildschirm(e)
(in classroom) die
Leinwand
(cinema) der Saal

sea das Meer(e), die See(n)
by the sea am Meer, an
der See
to the seaside ans Meer,
an die See
seafood die Meeresfrüchte
(pl)
sea salmon fillet das
Seelachs-Filet(s)
sea view der Seeblick(e)
season die Jahreszeit(en)
second zweite(n)
secondary school die
Hauptschule(n), die
Realschule(n)
to **sell** verkaufen
to **send** schicken
sender der Absender(-)
sentence der Satz("e)
September September
series die Serie(n)
serious ernstlich
serviette, napkin die
Serviette(n)
serving spoon der
Servierlöffel(-)
seven sieben
seventeen siebzehn
seventh siebte(n)
seventy siebzig
several, some einige
shame schade
she sie; es
to **shine** scheinen
shirt das Hemd(en)
shoe der Schuh(e)
shorthand Kurzschrift
shower die Dusche(n)
since seit
to **sing** singen
sister die Schwester(n)
site, plot of land das
Grundstück(e)
six sechs
sixteen sechzehn
sixth sechste(n)
sixty sechzig
to go **ski-ing** ski/fahren, ski//laufen
to **sleep** schlafen
(he/she/it sleeps er/sie/es
schläft)
slice die Scheibe(n)
small klein(e)
to **smell, stink** stinken
snack der Schnellimbiß
snack bar der
Schnellimbiß, die
Imbißstube(n)
snake die Schlange(n)
snow der Schnee
to **snow** schneien
it's **snowing** es schneit
so, thus so
so long as solange
social studies Sozialkunde
sofa das Sofa(s)
solution die Lösung(en)

some einige
sometimes manchmal
song das Lied(er)
sorry! Entschuldigung!
  I'm sorry es tut mir leid
to sort out sortieren
soup die Suppe(n)
south Süd
  in the south im Süden
  south Germany
  Süddeutschland
Spain Spanien
spare time die Freizeit
  in my spare time in meiner
  Freizeit
to speak sprechen
  (he/she/it speaks er/sie/es
  spricht)
speech bubble die
  Sprechblase(n)
to spend (money) (Geld)
  aus/geben
to spend (time) (Zeit) verbringen
to spend the night übernachten
spider die Spinne(n)
spirit der Geist(er)
spoon der Löffel(-)
sports club der Sportklub(s)
spring der Frühling
  in spring im Frühling
squash Squash
staircase, stairs die
  Treppe(n)
stamp die Briefmarke(n)
to stand stehen
to stare, goggle glotzen
station (main) der
  Hauptbahnhof
to stay, remain bleiben
stepbrother der Stiefbruder(")
stepfather der Stiefvater(")
stepmother die Stiefmutter(")
stepsister die
  Stiefschwester(n)
stick insect die
  Stabheuschrecke(n)
to stop halten
strawberry die Erdbeere(n)
street, road die Straße(n)
  on/in the street auf der
  Straße
  street children die
  Straßenkinder
  street theatre play das
  Straßentheaterstück(e)
strict streng
to stroll bummeln
student flat die
  Studentenwohnung(en)
studio discussion
  Studiodiskussion
stupid blöd, doof, dumm
subject (at school) das
  Fach("er)
such solche
sugar der Zucker
suit der Anzug("e)

summer der Sommer
  in summer im Sommer
sums of money die
  Geldsummen
sun die Sonne
  sun cream die
  Sonnencreme
  sun glasses die
  Sonnenbrille(n)
  sun shade der
  Sonnenschirm(e)
Sunday Sonntag
  on Sundays sonntags
surfboard das Surfbrett(er)
to go surfing surfen
surname, family name die
  Familienname(n)
survey die Umfrage(n)
sweet süß
  sweets die Bonbons, die
  Süßigkeiten (pl)
  sweethearts Liebhaber (pl)
to swim schwimmen
  to go swimming
  schwimmen gehen
  swimsuit der
  Badeanzug("e)
swine das Schwein(e)
swing boat die
  Schiffschaukel(n)
Swiss franc der Franken(-)
Swiss centime der Rappen(-)
Switzerland die Schweiz
symbol das Symbol(e)
symphony die Symphonie(n)

T

table, chart die Tabelle(n)
table der Tisch(e)
tablecloth die Tischdecke(n)
talk, gossip das Gerede
talk show die Talkshow(s)
to taste schmecken
  that tastes good
  das schmeckt gut
  that doesn't taste good
  das schmeckt nicht
tea der Tee
teacher die Lehrerin(nen), der
  Lehrer(-)
teaspoon der Teelöffel(-)
teenager der Teenager(s)
to telephone an/rufen
  telephone number die
  Telefonnummer(n)
television das Fernsehen, der
  Fernseher
  on television
  im Fernsehen
  television programme
  die Fernsehsendung(en)
tell me sag mal
temperature, degree der
  Grad
  what is the temperature?
  wieviel Grad ist es?

ten zehn
tennis Tennis
tennis racquet der
  Tennisschläger(-)
tent das Zelt(e)
terrace die Terrasse(n)
terraced house das
  Reihenhaus("er)
terrific, great köstlich, toll,
  prima
than als
thank you danke
that daß; das
the (m/f/n/pl) der/die/das/die
their ihr(e/n)
them sie
theme, subject das
  Thema(Themen)
then, next dann
then denn
  what are you doing then?
  was machst du denn?
there dort, da
therefore deshalb
they sie
thing die Sache(n)
to think (have an opinion)
  meinen
to think of denken an (+ Acc)
third dritte(n)
thirteen dreizehn
thirty dreißig
this, these diese
this evening heute abend
this is das ist
thousand tausend
three drei
thriller, crime series der
  Krimi(s)
through durch (+ Acc)
throwing the javelin der
  Speerwurf
Thursday Donnerstag
  on Thursdays donnerstags
time die Uhr; das Mal(e)
  what time is it? wieviel
  Uhr ist es? wie spät ist es?
  for the first time zum
  ersten Mal
  time of day die Uhrzeit
tip der Tip(s)
tired müde
title, caption der Titel
to nach (+ Dat); zu (+ Dat);
  in (+ Acc); an (+ Acc)
  to him/it ihm
toast der Toast(s)
together zusammen
toilet die Toilette(n)
tomato die Tomate(n)
tomato soup die
  Tomatensuppe
tomorrow morgen
tongue-twister der
  Zungenbrecher
too zu; (also) auch
  too old zu alt

too much zuviel
tortoise die Schildkröte(n)
total amount die Summe(n)
tourist der Tourist(en)
towel das Tuch(¨er); die Serviette(n)
trainers (shoes) die Turnschuhe (pl)
trampoline das Trampolin(e)
travel tips Reisetips (pl)
trousers die Hose(n)
trumpet die Trompete(n)
T-shirt das T-Shirt(s)
Tuesday Dienstag
on Tuesdays dienstags
tuneful, melodic melodisch
tunnel der Tunnel(s)
it's your **turn now!** jetzt bist du dran!
twelve zwölf
twenty twenty
two zwei; zweimal
two portions of chips zweimal Pommes (frites)
to **type** tippen
typing Maschinenschreiben
typing error der Tippfehler(-)
typical typisch

U

unbelievable, incredible unglaublich
uncle der Onkel
unhealthy ungesund
uninterrupted ununterbrochen
unlucky unglücklich
until bis
unusual, unusually ungewöhnlich
upright aufrecht
USA die USA, die Vereinigten Staaten (pl)

V

Valentine's Day der Valentinstag
valley das Tal(¨er)
vanilla die Vanille
one scoop of vanilla einmal Vanille
various verschieden
vegetables das Gemüse (sing.)
very sehr
Vienna Wien
village das Dorf(¨er)
violin die Geige(n)
vocabulary die Vokabeln (pl)
picture vocabulary Bildvokabeln (pl)
volleyball Volleyball

W

waistcoat die Weste(n)
to **wait for** warten auf (+ Acc)
waiter der Kellner(-)
waitress die Kellnerin(nen)
to **wake up** auf/wachen
Wales Wales
to **walk** gehen, spazieren/gehen
Walkman der Walkman
wallpaper die Tapete(n)
to **want to, wish to** wollen
wardrobe der Kleiderschrank(¨e)
warm warm
Warsaw Warschau
he/she/it **was** er/sie/es war
to **wash oneself** sich waschen
washing machine die Waschmaschine(n)
to **watch** gucken, sehen
to watch television fern/sehen, fern/gucken
water das Wasser
we wir
weather das Wetter
what is the weather like? wie ist das Wetter?
Wednesday Mittwoch
on Wednesdays mittwochs
week die Woche(n)
weekday der Alltag(e)
he/she/it **went** er/sie/es ging (from **gehen**)
they **went** sie gingen (from **gehen**)
west West
in the (wild) west im (Wilden) Westen
what? was?
what a shame wie schade!
what is your name? wie heißt du?
what are you saving up for? wofür sparst du dein Geld?
what do you think? was meinst du?
what is your house like? wie ist dein Haus
what kind of ...? was für ...?
when? wann?
where? wo?
where from? woher?
where to? wohin?
where are you going? wo fährst du hin?
which? welche(r/s)?
white weiß
Whitsuntide Pfingsten
who? wer?
window das Fenster(-)
windy windig
winter der Winter
in winter im Winter

wish der Wunsch
best wishes herzliche Grüße
with mit (+ Dat); bei (+ Dat)
are you coming with me? kommst du mit?
with it damit
woman die Frau(en)
wonderful wunderbar
wood der Wald(¨er)
word das Wort(¨er)
to **work** arbeiten; werken
pairwork die Partnerarbeit
first day of work der erste Arbeitstag
world die Welt
in the world auf der Welt
that **would be** das wäre
to **write** schreiben
write soon! schreib bald!
wrong falsch

Y

year das Jahr(e)
New Year Neujahr
New Year's Eve Sylvester
yes ja
yet doch, jedoch
yoghurt der Joghurt(s)
young jung
young person die/der Jugendliche
youth group die Jugendgruppe(n)
youth hostel die Jugendherberge(n)

Z

zero null

Auf welche Schule gehen diese Schüler?	Which school do these pupils go to?
Beantworte die Fragen.	Answer the questions.
Beschreib dein Haus/deine Wohnung/dich selbst.	Describe your house/flat/yourself.
Diese Sätze sind durcheinander.	These sentences are mixed up.
Finde die richtigen Antworten.	Find the right answers.
Füll die Lücken/die Sprechblasen aus.	Fill in the gaps/the speech bubbles.
Jetzt bist du dran!	Now it's your turn.
Kannst du andere ... schreiben?	Can you write other ... ?
Kannst du weitere Beispiele schreiben?	Can you write some more examples?
Kannst du andere Fragen stellen?	Can you ask other questions?
Lies den Brief/den Text/die Sätze.	Read the letter/the text/the sentences.
Mach dein eigenes Freizeitwappen.	Make your own 'leisure shield'.
Plane ein Picknick für vier Personen.	Plan a picnic for four people.
Schau im Wörterbuch nach.	Look in the dictionary.
Schlag in der Wörterliste nach.	Look in the vocabulary list.
Schreib ‚richtig' oder ‚falsch'.	Write 'true' or 'false'.
Schreib den Namen.	Write the name.
Schreib die (passenden) Namen/Preise auf.	Write out the (correct) names/prices.
Schreib die Sätze fertig.	Complete the sentences.
Schreib die Sätze in der richtigen Reihenfolge auf.	Write out the sentences in the correct order.
Schreib ein Zahlenrätsel/einen Brief.	Write a number puzzle/a letter.
Schreib folgende Sätze/die Antworten auf.	Write out the following sentences/the answers.
Sieh dir die Fotos/Bilder/Symbole/Texte an.	Look at the photos/pictures/symbols/texts.
Wähl den richtigen Satz/die passenden Uhrzeiten.	Choose the correct sentence/the correct times.
Was bedeuten die Namen der Dörfer?	What do the names of the villages mean?
Was bezahlen die Leute?	What do the people pay?
Was gehört zusammen?	What belongs together?
Was ist das beste ... für diese Personen?	What is the best ... for these people?
Was ist das?	What is that?
Was ist die Frage?	What is the question?
Was kostet alles?	What does everything cost?
Was machst du (gern)?	What do you (like to) do?
Was meinst du?	What do you think?
Was paßt zu wem?	What goes with whom?
Was sagen die Leute?	What do the people say?
Was sagst du am Schnellimbiß?	What do you say at the snack bar?
Welche Zahl ist das?	What number is it?
Welcher Text paßt zu welchem Bild/Foto?	Which text goes with which picture/photo?
Welcher Titel paßt am besten zu welchem Text?	Which title goes best with which text?
Welches Land ist das?	What country is it?
Welches Wort ist das?	What word is it?
Wer ist das/Nummer 1?	Who is it/number 1?
Wer sagt was?	Who says what?
Wie heißt ... ?	What is ... called? How do you say ... ?
Wie ist das richtig?	What is the right way/version?
Wie kann man hier essen und trinken?	What is the food and drink like here?
Wie schreibt man das richtig?	How is this written correctly?
Wieviel ist das (zusammen)?	How much is that (altogether)?
Wieviel macht das?	How much does that come to?
Wieviel Uhr ist es?	What time is it?
Wo liegen die Dörfer?	Where are the villages?
Wo liegt ... ?	Where is ... ?
Wo sind diese Leute?	Where are these people?
Wofür gibst du dein Geld aus?	What do you spend your money on?
Zeichne dein eigenes Poster für gesundes Essen.	Draw your own poster for healthy eating.